The First Year of College Teaching

D0829321

L. Dee Fink

NEW DIRECTIONS FOR TEACHING AND LEARNING
KENNETH E. EBLE, *Editor-in-Chief*

Number 17, March 1984

Paperback sourcebooks in
The Jossey-Bass Higher Education Series

WITHDRAWN

Jossey-Bass Inc., Publishers
San Francisco • Washington • London

L. Dee Fink.
The First Year of College Teaching.
New Directions for Teaching and Learning, no. 17.
San Francisco: Jossey-Bass, 1984.

New Directions for Teaching and Learning Series
Kenneth E. Eble, *Editor-in-Chief*

New Directions for Teaching and Learning is published quarterly
by Jossey-Bass Inc., Publishers. Subscriptions, single-issue
orders, change of address notices, undelivered copies, and other
correspondence should be sent to Subscriptions, Jossey-Bass Inc.,
Publishers, 433 California Street, San Francisco, California 94104.

Editorial correspondence should be sent to the Editor-in-Chief,
Kenneth E. Eble, Department of English, University of Utah,
Salt Lake City, Utah 84112.

Library of Congress Catalogue Card Number LC 83-82743
International Standard Serial Number ISSN 0271-0633
International Standard Book Number ISBN 87589-790-8

Cover art by Willi Baum
Manufactured in the United States of America

Ordering Information

The paperback sourcebooks listed below are published quarterly and can be ordered either by subscription or single-copy.

Subscriptions cost $35.00 per year for institutions, agencies, and libraries. Individuals can subscribe at the special rate of $21.00 per year *if payment is by personal check.* (Note that the full rate of $35.00 applies if payment is by institutional check, even if the subscription is designated for an individual.) Standing orders are accepted. Subscriptions normally begin with the first of the four sourcebooks in the current publication year of the series. When ordering, please indicate if you prefer your subscription to begin with the first issue of the *coming* year.

Single copies are available at $8.95 when payment accompanies order, and *all single-copy orders under $25.00 must include payment.* (California, New Jersey, New York, and Washington, D.C., residents please include appropriate sales tax.) For billed orders, cost per copy is $8.95 plus postage and handling. (Prices subject to change without notice.)

Bulk orders (ten or more copies) of any individual sourcebook are available at the following discounted prices: 10–49 copies, $8.05 each; 50–100 copies, $7.15 each; over 100 copies, *inquire.* Sales tax and postage and handling charges apply as for single copy orders.

To ensure correct and prompt delivery, all orders must give either the *name of an individual* or an *official purchase order number.* Please submit your order as follows:

Subscriptions: specify series and year subscription is to begin.
Single Copies: specify sourcebook code (such as, TL8) and first two words of title.

Mail orders for United States and Possessions, Latin America, Canada, Japan, Australia, and New Zealand to:
Jossey-Bass Inc., Publishers
433 California Street
San Francisco, California 94104

Mail orders for all other parts of the world to:
Jossey-Bass Limited
28 Banner Street
London EC1Y 8QE

New Directions for Teaching and Learning Series
Kenneth E. Eble, *Editor-in-Chief*

Contents

Introduction

The format of this *New Directions for Teaching and Learning* sourcebook differs from the customary format, which collects state-of-the-art essays from a variety of contributors. The decision to devote an entire issue to a single study of first-year teachers was prompted by the importance of the topic, the pertinence of the study in question, and the absence of close studies of the kind that it represents.

Developing New Teachers

Nothing is more important for the future of college teaching than the development of new teachers. Today, that development is seriously affected by the tight job market in many disciplines, which makes the profession less attractive and diminishes the number of new faculty coming into colleges and universities. The faculty development movement that grew significantly during the 1970s owed some of its strength to administrators' fears that a decrease in new appointments and an increase in tenuring-in could stagnate teaching faculties. Instead of relying on new faculty to provide new and current ideas, institutions would need to develop sources of stimulation within existing faculty.

One tentative conclusion this study has reached is that the beneficial impact of new faculty has probably been exaggerated. Most new teachers were not made quickly to feel a part of the college or university, few felt adequately supported by colleagues, and most were given heavy first-year teaching loads that limited their involvement in college activities outside the classroom. The belief that a normal flow of vibrant new faculty into a college maintains vitality is probably as erroneous as the belief that increasing the quantity of scholarship improves the quality of teaching. A sounder view of these complex matters, which data from this study suggest, is that both beginning and experienced faculty can be affected by institutional efforts to develop conditions, skills, attitudes, evaluations, and rewards favorable to teaching.

Common sense argues that such developments are likely to be better received and to produce greater results among faculty at the beginning of their career than among faculty who have reached a later stage. This does not mean that established teachers cannot develop teaching competence in many ways. The evidence from faculty development programs nationwide shows a very wide range of faculty participating in program activities. Examination of these programs indicates that the interaction of faculty — young and old, members of different disciplines, departments, and colleges — is one of the important ways

1

in which they make an impact. One salutary effect of a Lilly Endowment post-doctoral teaching fellows program in Indiana (Lacey, 1983) aimed at non-tenured junior faculty in their first years of teaching was that it also attracted participation from senior faculty.

Nevertheless, the study reported in this volume supports the advisability of using the beginning years to focus efforts to develop effective teachers. The data that it has produced can guide both formal faculty development efforts aimed at beginning teachers and the means by which new faculty are ordinarily introduced to their first position: "Having junior faculty find their place in the profession should be a major focus for any faculty development program" (Lacey, 1983, p. 101).

One interesting finding of the study reported here is that many first-year college teachers had inclinations and experience with teaching that preceded even their undergraduate years. For most college teachers, the chances are that commitment to a formal program of study grows out of long-term attraction and exposure to the teaching role. Many members of this group had also taken one or more education courses. Both predictably and sadly, the majority had a low opinion of such courses.

Taken together with the high value that these teachers placed on experience as a teaching assistant (and to a lesser degree on teaching experiences even prior to that), these findings warn against the fatal attraction of theory over practice. Professors of education are as prone to theorize as professors of any other subject; the unavoidable and unfavorable contrast between classroom theorizing about teaching and the living excitement of actual teaching does much to explain the low value given to education courses. Any group of graduate students or beginning teachers will vary widely in the amount of teaching experience that its members have had. Thus, if courses and teachers fail to recognize and adapt to these differences, some students will inevitably find formal instruction in teaching to be elementary, repetitious, and boring.

But, merely to single out junior faculty is not to guarantee the effectiveness of a faculty development program. The study reported here emphasizes some of the conditions—heavy teaching loads, the need to finish a dissertation, the lack of support from colleagues, the lack of information about teaching resources—that work to prevent a beginning faculty member from making a commitment to developing his or her teaching skills. In the Lilly Endowment program mentioned earlier, beginning faculty from the sciences were conspicuous by their absence. There seemed to be two reasons for this: emphasis placed on research in the sciences and the availability of postdoctoral fellowships to support research in the sciences (Lacey, 1983). In all disciplines and in the majority of universities, beginning faculty are not given light teaching loads. In major universities, only one in five of the teachers included in the present study thought that their teaching load was lighter than that of more experienced faculty, and two in five thought that their teaching load was heavier. Seventy-five percent of the respondents in all institutions thought that they were overloaded, although the response from any random selection of faculty might be similar.

Developing Good College Teachers

Perhaps the most important outcome of this study is the clues it provides to ways of developing good college teachers. Clearly, some measure of leisure to develop teaching skills is important in the beginning years. Clearly, a supportive atmosphere that values good teaching is important. Clearly, opportunities for and stimulation of interchange about teaching with others are important. Clearly, feedback about the specifics of teaching performance is important. Clearly, more sources of information and more readily available resources for effective teaching are important.

Any college and university can provide all these. However, the testimony of the representative group of beginning faculty included in this study indicates that such supportive measures are not much in evidence. Their absence is the more dismaying because the study was conducted in 1976–1978, after a considerable burst of faculty development activities.

Our surprise will be tempered if we look at the graduate school preparation of these prospective teachers. The project that culminated in this study was the Project on Teaching and Learning in Graduate Geography begun in 1973, which aimed at giving instructional training to graduate students. Geography is something of a latecomer to the efforts to improve the preparation of college teachers that went on in the graduate schools during the 1960s and early 1970s. All the major disciplines in the sciences were involved under National Science Foundation funding in commissions to improve undergraduate instruction. The commission in the biological sciences produced a monograph (Dean, 1970) that is a model of its kind. Any graduate department in which the preparation of teachers is a major responsibility could follow with profit its recommendations for ways of incorporating preparation for teaching into Ph.D. programs. More recently, groups in the disciplinary associations for economics and sociology have made efforts to improve the graduate school preparation of teachers.

The difficulty that all these programs face is one of diverting some portion of faculty and student intelligence and energies into the development of attitudes and skills necessary to effective teaching. Perhaps the overriding emphasis in the graduate schools on developing subject matter competence and research expertise in a specialized discipline creates that difficulty. The Commission on Undergraduate Education in the Biological Sciences (Dean, 1970) made some recommendations for improving the program for teaching assistants that could counter this emphasis, including the development of a course or seminar on effective teaching as a companion to teaching experience and enlistment of senior members in efforts to improve the program for future teachers. The declining market for college teachers has probably diverted attention away from efforts to develop teaching competence within graduate programs. For instance, competition for positions in the humanities has increased the pressure on graduate students to publish research even before they complete their graduate degree. In the battle for survival now going on in many disciplines in major universities, publish or perish is a major concern for new faculty members.

Preservice Preparation of College Teachers

Over the years, English departments have probably maintained more systematic efforts to develop graduate students as teachers than other departments have. The presence of a universitywide writing requirement and the disinclination of regular faculty to teach basic composition have necessitated a large corps of teaching assistants. Eble's (1972a, pp. 389–390) survey of programs and practices for preparing college teachers of English observed that, while English departments commonly provided specific pedagogic training and supervision, such efforts could be characterized as "largely defensive in nature. The need is to ensure some uniformity of practices among inexperienced teachers and to reduce the possible cries of outrage from students and parents and administrators." Then and now, few programs for teaching assistants look much beyond the rudimentary demands of the basic course.

The experience of the geography teachers in the study reported here probably reflects the common experience of teaching assistants. Ninety percent of the new teachers in this study had some experience as a teaching assistant, and about half said that they had had full responsibility for a class. "Experience is the best teacher," one wrote. "One learns what works and what doesn't." One third of the group had taken part in a special teaching preparation program. These new teachers had mixed but mildly positive reactions, many of which could be attributed to differences in their previous teaching experience. These new teachers also seemed to be more self-critical than the others, to perform comparatively well, and to derive somewhat more satisfaction from teaching during their first year than the others.

The preservice preparation of college teachers revealed in this study and by acquaintance with long-standing and prevailing practices in the graduate schools underlines the importance of in-service activities during the beginning years. The average graduate student may still be not much better prepared than the English professor (Lacey, 1983, p. 73) who recalled being invited to teach literature with two days' notice; the only advice that the appointing chairperson gave him was: "Don't worry. You will do well."

The difficulty in arguing that this casual approach must be improved is that some do well under it. The person whose experience has just been invoked is Walter Barker, now an associate professor at the University of Rhode Island. He developed into an excellent teacher. Still, he questions his method of induction, and he seeks to do better by the teaching assistants whom he now supervises. What he says of teaching assistants in English applies with equal force to other assistants: "As with the older faculty, a teaching assistant needs the time and resources to learn and practice teaching skills. And, he needs to do this while he is trying to pass his own courses, study for comprehensives, write a thesis or dissertation, pay rent, worry about loans and jobs, and struggle to maintain the appearance of sanity" (Lacey, 1983, p. 75). To apply Barker's remarks to beginning teachers, we need only to subtract passing courses and studying for comps and add preparing new classes, writing scholarly articles, serving on committees, and finding out how the new place works.

Conditions Facing New College Teachers

The simplest way of helping new college teachers to develop would be to reduce their teaching loads and to give them fewer different classes to teach during the first year. This is not a costly solution. The study reported here adds some needed precision about the effects of teaching load, class size, and number of different class preparations. The number of different class preparations seems to have the greatest negative impact. An obvious reason comes to mind: As an assistant, the new teacher has probably taught one basic course, but anything beyond that may be new ground. Although the data do not say so, we suspect that the new teachers who were assigned a number of different classes also had a large number of classes and students as well.

Still, the economic reason for giving beginning teachers a full teaching load is simple and compelling. Even if senior professors were not disinclined to teach beginning courses, the low cost of having new teachers teach such courses argues for the practice. However, team teaching arrangements in which the beginner either shared the load with a junior colleague or participated as a member of a larger team handling multisection courses are possible, and either arrangement could reduce the differences in costs that tend to place the responsibility for teaching large numbers of students in introductory courses on beginning teachers. The study reported here indicates that some team teaching is already taking place: While about only 40 percent of the new teachers reported being observed in a classroom by a colleague, half of the observations resulted from team teaching situations.

Eble's work with the Project to Improve College Teaching between 1969 and 1971 (Eble, 1972b) enabled him to visit some seventy representative colleges and universities across the country. The resulting impression about the ways in which new teachers begin their careers does not differ materially from that created by L. Dee Fink's study, nor has our work with faculty development of the the past ten years changed that impression.

In-Service Programs for New Teachers

Our impression is that few systematic programs exist to foster good teaching among the new arrivals on campus. The programs that do exist are more likely to be a part of a systematic effort at faculty development, which is often funded by outside sources, than they are to be an established institutional program. Although British colleagues have expressed some skepticism about the in-service training given to entering teachers in British universities, virtually all forty-six British universities provide a voluntary induction course for new staff members. According to Seldin (1977), approximately 70 percent of the new staff participate in the three- to four-day course. Still, in both British and American universities, there are few in-service opportunities for developing teaching skills.

Instead, at most American and British universities, an initial induction session or sessions is tied to periodic opportunities for discussions of teaching techniques, exposure to innovative methods, and information sessions designed to widen the new teacher's acquaintance with teaching resources. Informal social gatherings in which new faculty members get acquainted with one another and with current faculty are also common. Almost all such activities are voluntary, and participation depends heavily on the climate within the department, on the activities of department chairpersons and deans, and on the positive and negative pressures that a variety of sources exert.

At worst, much in the new faculty member's experiences goes against the development of teaching skills. As the present study documents, new faculty members are not customarily given the light teaching loads that favor the development of teaching skills. It is probably as true of other departments as it is of geography that the new teacher has a heavy load of classes and students, that the new teacher has to prepare a number of new courses, and that the new teacher is also struggling to finish a dissertation or get research publications under way. Although we have encountered no antisocial behavior toward new faculty members in our vists to many campuses at beginning-of-the-year exercises, social considerations rarely go beyond the invitation to dinner, the obligatory large gathering of faculty, and the informal socializing in which members of the new group establish friendships.

Responsibility for inclining new faculty members toward teaching excellence falls heavily on college and department administrators. Few administrators foster many activities beyond the obvious one — the day or half day devoted to introducing new staff and reviewing department operations and current business. Moreover, few administrators seem to recognize first-year problems and first-year opportunities to develop teaching skills when they make teaching assignments. Department chairpersons seem to receive little more induction into their specific tasks than beginning teachers do. While interest in faculty development seems to have led some administrators to increase their efforts to emphasize teaching at the beginning of the school year and to provide follow-up activities during the year for the benefit of new and experienced teachers alike, the glimpse of department and college operations offered by this study reveals little in the way of purposeful activities designed to develop teaching competence in beginning teachers.

Attitudes Toward Teaching and the Profession

A final word needs be said about attitudes and the reward system as they affect teaching. Many of the questions asked in this study disclose attitudes that can affect teaching in subtle but important ways. It is of more than passing interest that more than 80 percent of the participants accepted positively stated descriptions of student aptitudes and competence at the beginning of the year but that between one fourth and one half had a negative perception by midyear. This shift can be interpreted as the effect of the ordinary transition from the optimistic hopes that teachers entertain before a class begins to the pessimistic actualities that they soon encounter. However, at the extreme, a kind of destructive cynicism can take root in beginning teachers and be perpetuated throughout their career.

Moreover, 70 percent of the new teachers in the study reported here found a significant difference between the prevailing academic standards for students at the new institution and their own standards. A thoughtful faculty member should ponder the anxieties, confusion, and conflict that underlie their responses when they were asked how they dealt with this perceived difference: One half said that they maintained their standards, while the other half said that they lowered them. Once again, the study underlines the need for the exchange of insight and experience that a sensitive induction program can provide. The vertical movement between graduate school and full-time teaching is almost always downward. Princeton Ph.D.'s do not ordinarily begin teaching at Princeton. Great numbers of graduates from Harvard, Michigan, Johns Hopkins, and Stanford teach at Wabash, South Dakota State, Northeastern, and Bellevue College. There is no shame in it — indeed, there is much more opportunity than the beginning teacher is apt to recognize — and there is no just cause for disillusionment with students or for vain pride in one's own limited capacities. These are important lessons, and they are more likely to be learned in an atmosphere that encourages new teachers to examine the many complex questions that arise in the company of supportive colleagues.

The attitudes informing the satisfactions or dissatisfactions that beginning teachers experience are even more significant and even harder to assess. As with most occupations, the degree of satisfaction that one experiences has much to do with the quality of one's performance. Here, the data seem to confirm the truism that those who gain satisfaction from teaching teach better than those who do not. It could hardly be otherwise, since teaching is in part a performing art, and it steadily feeds on the interactions with those being taught. A number of respondents, about 10 percent, said that they planned to leave teaching after this first year. We do not know whether that figure is higher or lower than it should be for this or any other profession. We do know that those who leave have not put a long period of specialized study, considerable institutional resources, and a degree of sustained commitment to use as intended. In general, we know too little about students who fail or opt out. Instead, we tend to measure our success by our successes, which leads us to hold an overly favorable view of our enterprise.

Fewer than one half of the respondents in this study were certain that their institution's reward structure was favorable to excellence in teaching. The pattern was the expected one: Teachers in small undergraduate institutions thought that teaching was more fairly rewarded at their institutions than teachers in large graduate-oriented universities. Nevertheless, only 57 percent of the teachers in small institutions thought that the reward system encouraged good teaching and at major universities the proportion dropped to 46 percent. Only at five unidentified private universities did a solid majority, 80 percent, respond positively to this question.

The study does not pursue the reasons for these responses except to recognize that the common notion among new faculty was that attention to teaching was more a matter of lip service than it was real. However, if we reflect on the other data, some reasons become clear. The actualities that new teachers face give few indications of solid, enlightened support for teaching. As noted earlier, their teaching goes largely unobserved. While the shaky young teacher may welcome this fact, it does little to identify characteristics of effective teaching that might play a part in the reward system. Finally, a very small proportion of beginning teachers had found intellectual companionship among their colleagues — people with whom they could discuss ideas and professional concerns.

Although the data do not allow us to say that new faculty were isolated and alienated, they do say that few of these teachers had colleagues who were acquainted with and sympathetic to their aspirations and struggle. As a result, distrust of and anxieties about the reward system were inescapable.

Our conclusions about what this study reveals about teaching are both pessimistic and optimistic. Much that is easy to do is not being done, and what can be done at the cost of an extra expenditure of money, faculty energy and imagination, and administrative leadership has few chances of coming about. Our look at faculty development efforts at large inclines us to similar conclusions. As budgets tighten, such supposedly fringe activities as developing and fostering first-rate teaching go by the board. As a result, undergraduate colleges may be moving toward the situation that is now being roundly deplored in the public schools. That is, in competition with other professions, college teaching may attract increasingly fewer capable young men and women, and the greater values attached to research, consulting, outside recognition, and grantsmanship will be responsible. As in the public schools, teaching will become a safe place for middling competence, and it will supply only middling rewards.

Of course, this conclusion reads too much into a study that makes its own case on the range and specificity of its probing. The same data have another side that can only be encouraging to anyone who values teaching. The beginning teachers in the study did well in all the performance aspects that one might expect: They were successful in establishing good relations with students, their knowledge of the subject was sound, they were interested in self-evaluation, and they constructed tests that called for more than memorization. That as a group they did not do as well overall as experienced teachers should make experienced teachers feel good. That one sixth were above the average standards of even experienced teachers is not a bad percentage for first-year teachers. However, it is equally important that the majority said that they had experienced psychic satisfaction from teaching and that they planned to continue teaching. As the author of the study says, the psychic satisfaction derived from teaching may be the most precious asset that higher education has.

Kenneth E. Eble
John F. Noonan

References

Dean, D. *Preservice Preparation of College Biology Teachers.* Washington, D.C.: Commission on Undergraduate Education in the Biological Sciences, 1970.

Eble, K. E. "Preparing College Teachers of Engish." *College English,* 1972a, *33* (4), 385–406.

Eble, K. E. *Professors as Teachers.* San Francisco: Jossey-Bass, 1972b.

Lacey, P. A. (Ed.). *Revitalizing Teaching Through Faculty Development.* New Directions for Teaching and Learning, no. 15. San Francisco: Jossey-Bass, 1983.

Seldin, P. *Teaching Professors to Teach: Case Studies and Methods of Faculty Development in British Universities Today.* Croton-on-Hudson, N.Y.: Blythe-Pennington, 1977.

Kenneth E. Eble is professor of English at the University of Utah and editor-in-chief of New Directions for Teaching and Learning *(Jossey-Bass).*

John F. Noonan is dean, Iona College, New York, and past coeditor-in-chief of New Directions for Teaching and Learning *(Jossey-Bass).*

This study collected information about ninety-seven new college
teachers during their first year of college teaching. It provides
an empirical basis for understanding the initial development
of new professors as teachers.

Introduction to the Study

L. Dee Fink

In 1973, several academicians in the discipline of geography launched a nationwide project to give graduate students in geography who intended to enter the
academic profession training in instructional skills. Eventually, the Project
on Teaching and Learning in Graduate Geography (TLGG) became a
consortium of programs in sixteen Ph.D.-granting departments of geography
in the United States. The directors of these programs offered seminars on college teaching, supervised various types of practicum, and organized retreats
or orientation programs on college teaching (Pattison and Fink, 1974).

In time, it was asked whether these activities were in fact accomplish-
ing what they were intended to do; namely, to allow participating graduate
students to develop ideas and skills that would enable them to teach more effectively than they otherwise would. As associate director of the national project, I
proposed a study that would compare the teaching of new teachers who participated in the preparatory programs with the teaching of new teachers from the
same discipline who did not participate. The study was funded by the National
Science Foundation. At about the same time, both I and others realized that the
study gave us a chance to learn much more than whether the TLGG programs
had been effective. That is, it was also an opportunity to learn about the more
general process of starting a career in the academic profession.

This new perspective on the study generated some new kinds of questions that were more fundamental and larger in scope than the ones first envisioned. What kinds of background experiences did the new teachers have that

L. D. Fink. *The First Year of College Teaching.* New Directions for Teaching
and Learning, no. 17. San Francisco: Jossey-Bass, March 1984.

might have prepared them for college teaching? What effect did these prior experiences have on their performance? What kinds of situations did the new teachers face when they started to teach? What did they try to do as a teacher in a college or university? How well did they perform during their first year? How did they feel about their first year as a full-fledged academic? What effect did these feelings have on their future career plans? While these new questions significantly enhanced the value of the study, they still had to be investigated within the framework of the study as proposed and funded.

Structure of the Study

The research grant provided the resources to study 100 beginning college teachers. Because of the relatively small number of graduates each year in the discipline of geography, the study was extended over a period of two academic years, 1976–77 and 1977–78. This made it possible to identify fifty new teachers each year with the necessary characteristics.

Selecting the Study Population. To obtain a sample of 100 new teachers, I contacted thirty Ph.D.-granting departments of geography, half of which had participated in the TLGG project. These departments varied in quality and prestige, but by and large they were the better-known departments in the country. These thirty departments gave me the names of 266 graduates, 117 (44 percent) of whom were eligible for participation in the study. Of those eligible, 105 agreed to participate, and 97 completed the study.

In order to be eligible for inclusion, the graduate student needed both to have succeeded in obtaining an academic appointment that year and not to have taught at the college level for a significant number of years before entering the doctoral program.

Types of Information Collected. With the exception of information that I collected on several site visits as research director, the information used in this study was collected by questionnaire. Because many kinds of relationships were being studied, many kinds of information were needed. Six types of information, representing the six aspects of career development to be examined, were needed. These are listed below, followed by examples of questions soliciting that kind of information.

Behavior

Did you evaluate your teaching in any formal or quasi-formal manner during the past half year?

(For the students: Did the teacher promote teacher-student discussions?)

Perceptions

What type of teacher do you see yourself as, that is, as following the principles-and-facts prototype, the instructor-centered prototype, the student-as-mind prototype, or the student-as-person prototype?

Do you perceive students at your college or university to be different in any general way from students at other institutions? If so, in what way?

Intentions

What types of learning activities do you intend to use this year? What changes in your professional activity do you plan to make next year?

Situations

How many courses have you been assigned to teach this year? Do you have a tenure-track or non–tenure-track appointment?

Feelings

To what degree have your experiences as a teacher this year produced professional satisfaction for you?

Would you have liked more support from your colleagues this year? If so, what kinds of support?

Judgments

How would you rate your own performance as a lecturer, as a discussion leader, this year?

(For the teacher's colleagues: How would you compare the participant's performance as a college teacher this year to that of other beginning college teachers you have known?)

Sources of Information. Information was obtained from four different sources: beginning teachers, their students, three colleagues, and the research director. Each participating teacher completed four different questionnaires. A questionnaire seeking background information was completed before the academic year began. The other three were completed near the beginning, middle, and end of the academic year respectively. Next, all participating teachers were asked to have students in at least one of their courses complete a course evaluation instrument. Forty-six new teachers had evaluations in two or more sections or courses. To obtain information from their colleagues, a questionnaire was sent near the end of their academic year to the chairperson and to two other colleagues in their department. Finally, as director of this research project, I made on-site visits to the campuses of thirty participants to interview them and to visit at least one of their classes.

General Assessment of the Research Data

To the best of my knowledge, this is the most comprehensive study of beginning college teachers that has been conducted to date. Although the number of subjects is not exceptionally large, this is the only study that has used multiple sources of information to collect direct, person-specific information about the origins, situation, and performance of even a moderate number of new teachers. Nonetheless, the research data have some limits as well as some advantages, and these need to be noted at the outset.

Number of Disciplines Included. The fact that the subjects are all members of one academic discipline is both a disadvantage and an advantage. In one sense, it would have been preferable to include a large number of subjects from all disciplines or at least from all major disciplines. However, this would have made the study much more expensive, and it would have created problems of making comparisons between disciplines.

The fact that all subjects were from a single discipline reduced the cost, simplified the sampling procedure, and made comparisons possible within the complete sample. Another advantage is that this particular discipline is multifaceted; that is, part of it is similar to the natural sciences, part is similar to the social sciences, and part is similar to the humanities (Broeck, 1965). This means that the discipline probably shares a number of teaching problems with other disciplines. It also means that the results can be generalized with more confidence than would have been justified with perhaps any other discipline.

However, the majority both of the questions raised and of the relationships studied do not appear to depend primarily on the nature of the discipline. For example, the ability of a faculty member to assess the needs and capabilities of students, to gather the support and confidence of colleagues, or to organize meaningful learning activities seem in all likelihood to depend more on the general nature and structure of higher education than on the peculiar characteristics of the particular discipline. Hence, I feel confident that the results of the sample used in this study can, with but few qualifications, safely be generalized to the situation and experiences of most beginning college teachers in American higher education today.

Single Focus of the Study. Although questions were asked about many types of academic activities, including research and advising, the primary concern was teaching. The intention was not to denigrate the other functions of college teachers, since they are all important. It is just that I was most concerned with college teaching. An understanding of the academic activities will have to wait on other studies.

Period of Time Covered. The fact that the study covered only the first year of teaching was both an asset and a limitation. That it covered a whole year made it much more informative than a study of a single course or even of a semester. That it covered only one year, not three or five, means that it cannot be taken as a study of the entire developmental period of the academic career. Nonetheless, the one year studied was sufficient to reveal relationships not identified in the existing research literature.

Sample Size. The sample of new teachers used in this study was restricted in the sense that its members were graduates of thirty of the fifty-two Ph.D.-granting departments in this discipline. However, the thirty departments that were selected represented the better-known departments and institutions in the United States. Hence, it seems plausible to assume that the individuals studied are reasonably representative of the college teachers being produced by American graduate education today.

Although the number of graduate departments involved was limited, the proportion of graduating doctoral students who participated in the study was high. Of the graduates who were eligible and able to be contacted, 83 percent agreed to participate and completed the study. Hence, the study can be viewed as a nearly comprehensive sample from thirty carefully selected departments.

Response Rate. As already noted, almost all the information collected was collected from questionnaires. The success rate in obtaining the requested information was high. Overall, 96 percent of the questionnaires solicited — four from participants, three from colleagues, one course evaluation from students — were received. This means that the file of information was essentially complete for every participant in the study. The only significant exception is that, for 21 percent of the participants, questionnaires were received from only two colleagues, not from three.

Course Evaluation Instrument. The instrument used to evaluate the courses taught by participants was a critical aspect of this study. It was essential to obtain good information in this area, since we were attempting to understand what was happening to the participants as teachers. To obtain this information, it was necessary for all participants to use the same method of evaluation, although they worked at different institutions. This requirement ruled out the possibility of allowing participants to use their own institutional system of evaluation. It also seemed preferable to use an instrument that had been carefully developed and refined for general purposes, not one designed only for this study.

As a result of these considerations, a decision was made to use the IDEA (Instructional Development and Effectiveness Assessment) system developed at Kansas State University by Donald Hoyt (Hoyt and Cashin, 1977). It has several attractive features. First, its central concern is whether the students learned what the professor was trying to teach. This is its biggest advantage over other commercially available course evaluation instruments. Second, its norms for comparison are large and nationwide. Third, its norms and comparisons take class size and student motivation level into account. Fourth, it has an unusual diagnostic component that could be helpful to participants.

I also had to decide which courses to evaluate. To evaluate every course taught by every participant would have made the analysis very unwieldy. Hence, I decided to ask participants to use the IDEA instrument in their largest course. The reason for this decision was simply that, since a choice had to be made, the largest course was the one in which the teacher affected the largest number of students.

As a check, some participating teachers were asked to use this instrument more than once to see whether the results varied significantly. Forty-six participants used it more than once—with multiple sections of the same course, with different courses, or with the same course at different times. The results of this check on consistency are presented in Chapter Four.

Multiple Perspectives. One of the most significant and positive aspects of this study was that multiple perspectives were available on several questions. As a result, it was possible to examine the answers of different respondents to particular questions. For example, it was not necessary to rely solely on student evaluation scores to measure teaching effectiveness. It was possible to ask how each teacher was perceived by students, by colleagues, and by the teacher himself or herself, then to make comparisons.

Summary

This study collected data over the course of one full year on ninety-seven new college teachers in the discipline of geography. It focused primarily on their activity as teachers. While these characteristics imposed certain limits on the study, they also facilitated analysis. Three other characteristics significantly enhanced the quality of the data obtained in the study: the high response rate, the quality of the course evaluation instrument, and the multiple sources of information.

L. Dee Fink works in the Office of Instructional Services at the University of Oklahoma as instructional consultant for the teaching faculty there, a position that he has held since 1979. Prior to that, he was associate national director of the the Project on Teaching and Learning in Graduate Geography, and he held a joint appointment in the department of geography and the College of Education at the University of Oklahoma.

The new teachers had had a variety of personal and formal educational experiences before they began teaching. This chapter describes the extent of several of these experiences and the effect they had on the new teachers in their first year.

The Backgrounds of the New Teachers

L. Dee Fink

Before people in this study started teaching at the college level, they had a variety of personal and professional experiences that prepared (or failed to prepare) them for college teaching. This chapter describes these experiences, analyzes their effect on the first year of teaching, and describes the sorting process — the academic selection procedures that determine who goes where.

Characteristics of Participants

Age and sex breakdowns for the study population as are follows:

Age		*Sex*	
21–25	4%	Male	88%
26–30	46	Female	12
31–35	43		
36 +	6		

It is difficult to assess the representativeness of these characteristics. A study by McCall and others (1961) contains an age breakdown for new faculty members in institutions with an enrollment of 3,000 students or less. This break-

L. D. Fink. *The First Year of College Teaching.* New Directions for Teaching and Learning, no. 17. San Francisco: Jossey-Bass, March 1984.

down shows a greater age spread. The data in the present study probably reflects a change in the character of faculty recruitment since the early 1960s. The proportion of new female faculty members in this study (12 percent) is much lower than the proportion of female assistant professors nationwide (32 percent). But geography is traditionally a male-dominated discipline: Only 9 percent of academic geographers of all ranks are female, while the comparable figure nationwide for all disciplines combined is 25 percent ("AAG Membership Profiles," 1979; *Fact Book on Higher Education*, 1977). Looking at changes over time, then, it appears that American faculty members today come from a narrower age range and that the proportion of female faculty members is slowly increasing.

Table 1 summarizes the formal education of study participants. It justifies a number of observations. First, very few participants received an Associate of Arts degree before continuing their higher education. This may mean that few junior college graduates enter the academic career, or it may mean that geography is not well represented in most junior colleges. Second, most study participants had already selected geography or a related subject as their major during their undergraduate years. This means that decisions about the field that these people finally entered were made at a fairly early stage in their education. Third, most participants were undergraduates during the tumultuous late 1960s, and they were graduate students during the quieter 1970s.

Table 1. Formal Education of the Study Population

	Degree Level			
	A.A.	B.A./B.S.	M.A./M.S.	Ph.D.
Percentage Receiving the Degree	7%	100%	100%	100%
Major				
Geography	1%	63%	91%	96%
Geography related (social sciences, history, geology)	0	17	6	4
Other (English, business, education)	6	12	3	0
Year Graduated				
Median year	1964	1969	1972	1977
Institutional Source of Support				
State	6%	74%	83%	78%
Private	1	23	14	22
Denominational	0	2	3	0
Size of Institution				
Median enrollment	20,000	14,500	23,000	30,000
Number who received this degree outside the U.S.	0	16	7	0

This means that they experienced two very different types of campus atmosphere, but the effect of these atmospheres on their own attitudes probably varied from person to person. Fourth, most participants attended a state-supported institution for the duration of their career in higher education, as most American students (78 percent) do. In this sense, they are representative of the mainstream of the American student body. Fifth, one in six received his or her B.A. or B.S. degree in a foreign country and came to the United States to do graduate work. Nearly all these participants came from countries that are present or former members of the British Commonwealth. Six of these sixteen participants returned to their home country to teach, but the other ten stayed here, where they contributed to the internationalization of American faculty.

Learning How to Teach

There are two very different perspectives on the origin of good teaching. Each perspective was held by some participants in this study. One view, which can be labeled the *talent view*, sees an individual's teaching performance as depending on the individual's God-given talent and on the amount of time that he or she puts into it. The other view, which can be labeled the *developmental view*, sees an individual's teaching performance at any given time as reflecting his or her stage of development as a teacher at that time. Development consists of an increasing understanding of the subject matter, of oneself as a knower and teacher, of students, and of the processes of teaching and learning.

Since this study is based on the second view, I asked participants the questions that follow from it: When did they decide to become a college teacher? When did they decide that they wanted to teach this subject matter? What people were influential in that decision and in shaping their view of good teaching? How much and what kinds of prior teaching experience did they have? How much and what kinds of formal training did they have for college teaching? How valuable had that experience and training been in helping them to develop the understanding and skills necessary for good teaching? Their responses to these questions are summarized in the sections that follow.

The Decision to Become a College Teacher. The participants varied greatly in terms of when and how they had decided to become a college teacher. During the interviews, several remembered deciding that they wanted to teach while they were in high school or even in grade school. For them, it was only a question of the subject to teach and the level at which to teach. Others did not make the decision until they were in college or even in graduate school. The members of this group discovered an attraction for the subject matter first, then decided to teach it rather than to work with it in some other role.

Many participants mentioned individual teachers who had been especially influential in their decision. These participants seemed to want to do for others what these teachers had done for them, whether this meant making a subject come alive, demonstrating the potential of an individual mind, or something else. I did not expect the frequency with which participants mentioned the significance of parents who were teachers and of teaching in situations other than school. Unfortunately, the role of parents emerged only in the interviews, and I did not notice it early enough to gather systematic information on it through the questionnaires. However, participants did have a chance to comment on teaching experiences in settings other than school, and nearly half identified some such experience, which ranged from such things as teaching sailing during the summer to fulfilling one of the many teaching roles in Mormon society. Many comments suggested that, during these other teaching occasions, people saw themselves as doing something well and as liking it. This attracted them to the role of teaching and eventually to the profession of teaching.

Experiences and Training Prior to Graduate School. As Table 2 shows, a large portion of the participants (47 percent) had had some kind of teaching experience before they entered graduate school, either in grade school (4 percent), high school (24 percent), or college (33 percent). (The individual figures sum to more than 47 percent because some participants had taught at more than one level.) These figures are similar to those obtained in a survey of college teachers by Eckert and Williams (1972). These authors found that 23 percent of the faculty at the University of Minnesota had had public school teaching experience and that 37 percent of the faculty in four-year colleges had been elementary or secondary school teachers. When participants in our study were asked how significant their prior teaching experience had been to their development as teachers, they rated it quite high: 2.98 on a scale of 0–4.

A large portion of participants (35 percent) had also taken one or more education courses, and more than half of these participants had taken four or more such courses. However, the majority had a low opinion of these courses: The average rated significance of education courses was 1.21. (scale 0–4). Here are two typical comments: "Most were awful. They almost caused me not to be a teacher." "I started taking an education course and found I wasn't learning doodly squat, so I quit." Most of the very few positive comments referred to student teaching experiences, not to course work. Here is one typical comment: "[The education courses were] not particularly significant except student teaching. That was important in confronting the realities of the classroom situation and applying materials of other courses."

Experiences and Training During Graduate School. The most significant experience during graduate school, both in frequency and in rated value, was that of being a teaching assistant (TA). As Table 2 shows, eighty-seven participants (90 percent) said that they had been a TA during graduate school and 54 of this number said that they had had full responsibility for a class. Their comments indicated that participants were by and large appreciative of the chance to teach.

Table 2. Prior Teaching Experience and Education Courses: Amount and Rated Significance

	Percentage of Respondents	Rated Significance
Before Graduate School		Scale: 0 [low] to 4 [high]
Elementary school	4%	
Taught 1 year	4%	
Secondary school	24%	2.98
Taught 1 year	15%	
Taught 2 to 7 years	9%	
College/University	33%	
Taught 1 or 2 years	18%	
Taught 3 to 8 years	15%	
Education Courses	35%	1.21
1 to 4 courses	15%	
5 or more courses	20%	
During Graduate School		
Teaching assistantship	90%	3.17
1 or 2 times	11%	
3 or 4 times	17%	
5 or more times	62%	
Full responsibility for a course	56%	
Partial responsibility for a course	34%	
Education courses	8%	1.38
Teaching outside the department	37%	2.94
1 or 2 times	15%	
3 or 4 times	7%	
5 or more times	15%	

"Experience is the best teacher; one learns what works and what doesn't work."

"At [my graduate school], advanced graduate students [Ph.D. candidates] are given almost total responsibility for teaching introductory courses in physical and cultural geography — an invaluable experience, since most Ph.D.'s in the discipline end up in academia as teachers."

However, participants also expressed reservations that the opportunity had not been all that it might have.

"A TA at [my graduate school] was rarely given increased responsibility with seniority. Hence, the job became rather dull after the first year or so."

"No conscious effort by faculty to teach graduate TAs different methods of teaching. Thus, it was a learn-by-yourself situation."

"Very useful for seminar-type teaching, but [it] gave insufficient experience in lecturing."

The general desire seemed to be for a gradual increase in responsibility, with help along the way but with freedom and autonomy, too, especially at the end.

A second major opportunity to learn about teaching came when participants taught outside the department while they were still in graduate school. This happened for thirty-six participants. Usually, this experience came from extension programs, another department on campus, evening school, or a nearby smaller college. Participants gave it high ratings for its contribution to their development as teachers: The average rated significance was 2.94 on a scale of 0–4. This high rating may relate to the fact that it is a high-gain low-risk situation. Unlike some TA positions, it presented participants with the full range of teaching responsibilities: syllabus preparation, choice of reading material, preparation of classes, lecturing, leading discussions, preparing tests, and assigning grades. It was low-risk because their performance was by and large unknown to the graduate advisers who evaluated them and wrote letters of reference. The experience may also have been helpful because it placed them in institutions and departments that had a different social-ethical system; that is, in institutions and departments that placed the primary value on teaching and students, not on research and the discipline. This might have been especially helpful for those who went on to teaching-oriented departments.

Special Teaching Preparation Programs. Thirty participants had taken part in a special teaching preparation program offered by their department while they were a graduate student — the TLGG programs described in Chapter One. Each department offered its own set of activities, but this set usually included four or more of the activities shown in Figure 1. We were particularly interested in learning whether participants who took part in such programs perceived them as having been effective now that they were teaching.

When asked how they would rate the significance of these activities in their own development and performance as a teacher during the year when they participated in our study, six replied that the activities had had a strong positive effect, ten said that they had had a moderate positive effect, while fourteen said that they had not had much effect one way or the other. No one said that such activities had had a negative effect. Thus, the general reaction can be described as mildly positive.

A close analysis of participants' comments both in the questionnaires and in the interviews yields some reasons for the mild response and suggests that the main benefit from participation in such programs may not come until after the first year of teaching. First, some of the negative reaction seemed to result from an interaction effect with certain individuals. Thus, it was not were quite outspoken in their reaction. For example:

Figure 1. Basic Teaching Preparation Activities and Their General Function

Activity	Function
Teaching a course Miniteaching Developing plans and materials for a course	Provides experience
Having one's teaching diagnosed by an observer Observing oneself teach	Provides feedback
Observing others teach	Provides models
Readings and lectures about teaching and learning Discussions about teaching and learning	Develops one's conceptualization of the act of teaching

Source: Fink (1976–77).

inherent in the nature of the programs themselves. Some participants were quite outspoken in their reaction. For example:

"[I participated in] the department's seminar on teaching for one quarter. It was a total waste of time."

However, other participants from the same graduate department who had taken part in exactly the same program felt quite positive about their experience. Hence, it would be a mistake to conclude that the programs were bad. It would be more accurate to conclude that the programs were not helpful for all participants.

Second, some participants offered a number of reasons for the failure of preparation programs to affect them personally. Four comments illustrate the most significant criticisms:

"I already had six years of teaching experience when I entered graduate school. These activities didn't teach me anything I didn't already know." Many detractors of the programs had had prior teaching experience.

"The discussions we had on 'how to' did not lead to anything beyond what one would come to with a little common sense and sensitivity." That is, the programs provided no significant new insights.

"[The director of the program] did not challenge my basic ideas; he only reinforced what I already knew and believed in."

"[Most analysis of our teaching] was in terms of superficials — mannerisms, style, and so forth." That is, the analysis was shallow.

Third, participants who did find participation helpful frequently referred to a more developed interest in teaching and to a fuller awareness of options and factors to be considered. Three comments are illustrative:

"The TLGG program increased my overall interest in improving my teaching skills, that is, my ability to give lectures, lead labs, and write good exams. And, it increased my interest in teaching per se."

"The discussions forced me to verbalize my approach to teaching and my reasons for doing what I do. As a result, I am now more conscious and deliberate in thinking about what I do as a teacher."

"The thing I enjoyed about the program was that I was not the only one trying to learn about teaching; there was a group of people, all of whom were trying things and talking about it. This made it very exciting."

There seemed to be special value in the experience of working with a single professor on a given course for a whole semester or year before being given full responsibility for a course as a TA. Not many people had this opportunity, but all those who did found it very worthwhile, as this comment shows:

"[During the several quarters in which I worked with this professor] I received advice and part-time classroom experience. From the examples I saw, I realized the need for organized preparedness, enthusiasm, diversity of delivery (use of slides, films, maps, and so forth) and respect in the classroom deriving both from these things and from genuine interest in students."

Fourth, one respondent made an important observation explaining why he thought that his participation in the TLGG program had not affected his teaching much in the current year but that it would in the future:

"The program made me aware of different teaching options and made me think about them. The problem is that this year, between teaching several new courses and finishing my dissertation, I simply don't have the time to work up or try these other options. Hence, I think the real payoff will come in another year or two down the line."

In conclusion, it is clear that some people did not find the TLGG teaching preparation programs to be very helpful, at least not during their first year of teaching. For some, the reason lay in the perceived shortcomings of particular programs. For others, it lay in the nature of the participants themselves; that is, prior teaching experience precluded a major impact. However, more than half of the participants did find that the programs were helpful. Moreover, there is reason to believe that the new ideas about teaching that they acquired might be productive once the frenzy of the first year of teaching had passed.

Effects of Earlier Experiences on the First Year. Because all the data in this study are person-specific, it is possible to ask whether new teachers who had a particular kind of experience or training before they began teaching were systematically different during their first year than those who lacked such experience or training. Table 3 contains breakdown statistics showing the effects of experiences prior to and during graduate school on the participants' sense of readiness for college teaching, on the quality of their teaching as measured by three different types of evaluation, and on the professional satisfaction that they felt at the end of their first year of teaching.

All the experiences prior to graduate school seemed to have had a positive effect. The education courses and precollegiate teaching experiences had an especially strong effect on the participants' sense of readiness and on their self-assessment. Those who had taught in grade school and high school were basically confident that they could also teach well at the college level. By and large, the performance data supported their belief.

There was also a strong positive relationship between the amount of earlier nonacademic teaching experience and the participants' sense of readiness and performances. It may be that these experiences helped them to enjoy and gain confidence in their teaching role outside schools and that this helped them subsequently in the classroom.

During graduate school the experience of being a teaching assistant seemed to help participants improve in respect to all three factors: readiness, performance, and satisfaction. However, those who taught courses ourside their graduate department had significantly higher student evaluations, higher even than those of the TAs who had had full responsibility for courses. This datum supports the high perceived value that the participants had of teaching outside the department.

There was one unusual effect related to participation in the TLGG teaching preparation programs. Although the relationships are not linear, those who participated in these programs and valued them did comparatively well on performance as rated by colleagues and students and they found a reasonable amount of satisfaction in teaching during their first year. However, they had a lower sense of readiness, and their self-evaluations were also significantly lower. One possible inference is that participation in these programs affected their awareness of the demands and possibilities of good teaching more than it affected their ability to implement these possibilities, at least during the first year.

The General Effect of Prestigious Graduate Departments. Some have speculated that graduates of highly rated graduate departments are more talented in some general sense and that they are better at both teaching and research as a result. The data from this research, combined with information

Table 3. Breakdown of Readiness, Performance, and Satisfaction by Amount of Prior Teaching Experience and Education Courses

Experiences Prior to Graduate School	Self-Assessed Readiness Scale: (10–33)	Performance, as Assessed by:			Satisfaction with First Year (1–5)	(N)
		Self (0–4)	Colleagues (0–4)	Students (1–100)		
1. Education Courses						
0 courses	23[c]	2.8[c]	2.8	30	3.7	59
1–4 courses	24	2.9	2.8	38	4.1	18
5 or more courses	26	3.4	3.0	41	4.1	20
2. Precollegiate Teaching						
0 years	23[c]	2.8[b]	2.9[a]	32	3.9	71
1–2 years	25	3.2	2.7	38	3.8	22
3 years or more	26	3.0	3.6	48	4.3	4
3. College-Level Teaching						
0 years	23[a]	2.9	2.9	33	3.8	66
1–2 years	24	3.0	3.0	49	4.1	17
3 years or more	25	3.0	2.7	23	4.0	14
4. Other (nonacademic) Teaching?						
No	23[b]	2.9[b]	2.8[a]	31[b]	3.8	77
Yes	25	3.2	3.1	44	4.0	20

Experiences During Graduate School

1. T.A. Experiences					
none	22[b]	2.8	2.6	25	3.3	10
T.A.: partial responsibility	23	2.9	2.9	38	4.0	33
T.A.: full responsibility	24	3.0	2.9	33	3.9	54
2. Teaching Outside Department					
0 times	23[a]	2.9	2.8	28[c]	3.8	59
1–2 times	23	2.9	3.2	32	4.1	15
3–4 times	23	3.0	2.6	61	3.8	16
5 times or more	26	3.3	2.9	48	4.2	15
3. Teaching Preparation Program					
Not Available	23	3.1[c]	2.9	37	3.9	55
Not Participated	25	3.2	2.6	39	3.6	12
Not Valued	24	2.6	2.7	28	3.9	14
Participated and Valued	23	2.7	3.2	33	3.9	16

Note: In a one-way analysis of variance, the difference among the means are significant at a probability level of:
a = 0.10
b = 0.05
c = 0.01

from two published reports that rank departments of geography nationally, make it possible to evaluate this hypothesis, at least for this discipline. A survey by Roose and Andersen (1970) asked practitioners to rank doctoral departments in order of status. Hence, this survey really measured prestige. Another ranking was done by the department of geography at Syracuse University (Sopher and Duncan, 1975). Assuming that a "better" department would never hire graduate students from a "lesser" department, these investigators examined the placement of graduate students on their first appointment and rank-ordered departments accordingly. The correlation between these two ratings is high, + .84.

For each of the two surveys, the thirty graduate departments where participants in this study did their graduate work can be divided into three groups of ten members each. Next, we can compare the average teaching performance of graduates of these three groups as measured by three criteria. The results of this comparison are displayed in Table 4.

Although the differences are not great, the graduates of the more prestigious departments did not teach quite as well as a group as the graduates of the less prestigious departments. There was a slight negative correlation (– 0.15 and – 0.14 for the two rankings respectively) between the prestige of the participant's graduate department and his or her subsequent teaching performance.

Who Went Where?

The sorting process whereby the graduate student from one institution eventually becomes a college teacher at another institution is a complex but not a random process. A number of patterns are followed. These patterns have been examined for the participants in this study with respect to three factors: institutional prestige, type of institution, and geographic movement.

Institutional Prestige. Are graduate students from prestigious universi-

Table 4. Do Graduates of Prestigious Departments Teach Better?

		Teaching Performance as Measured by:	
	Self-Assessment Scale: 0-4	Colleague Assessment 0-4	Student Assessment 1-100
Prestige of Graduate School as Measured by: *Roose and Andersen (1970)*			
First 10	2.9	2.7	32
Second 10	2.9	3.0	36
Third 10	3.1	2.9	35
Prestige of Graduate School as Measured by: *Sopher and Duncan (1975)*			
First 10	2.9	2.8	33
Second 10	2.9	2.8	31
Third 10	3.0	3.0	41

ties hired by other elite universities, are they hired by somewhat less prestigious universities, or do they disperse evenly among all types of institutions? In the early 1940s, Logan Wilson (1942) claimed that graduate students who enter academic work find a position in an institution that is somewhat lower on the prestige hierarchy than the institution at which they did their graduate work. Several years later, when higher education was entering a period of rapid expansion, Caplow and McGee (1958, p. 212) thought that major universities were "holding more of their graduates at their own level, trading them with one another and employing them at home rather than supplying them to the minor leagues, which in turn supply them to the bush leagues."

What happened during the late 1970s when enrollments in higher education had leveled off and when in some years they were actually declining? Figure 2 shows the movement along the prestige hierarchy for participants in our study as measured by the national rankings of Roose and Andersen (1970). Only one participant went to a department ranked higher than the one from which she came, while twenty-two went to a department of similar rank, and sixty-four went to a department that ranked lower on the Roose and Andersen hierarchy.

The general pattern resembles the type described by Wilson (1942): People move down the hierarchy but not very far down. More than half (55 percent) of the participants in this study did their doctoral work in one of the top fifteen departments, while 80 percent went on to a department that was ranked lower but that still had some graduate programs.

Type of Institution. When I examined the characteristics of the departments and institutions where new teachers accepted their first appointment in terms other than prestige, there was somewhat more dispersion, but there was still a dominant trend. As Table 5 shows, most participants accepted an appointment in a large state-supported graduate institution with large graduate degree–granting departments. Hence, many went to departments and institutions that had some of the characteristics of the institution at which they did their final graduate work.

Geographic Movement. A significant amount of geographic movement was involved in the first academic appointment. Of the ninety-seven participants, seventy-two crossed a state boundary, fifty crossed a regional boundary (as defined by the regions used by the National Center for Education Statistics), and ten crossed an international boundary. This geographic movement not only had financial significance, but it was also a factor in the social and cultural adjustment that participants had to make, a factor which will be examined further in the next chapter.

How Are Candidates Chosen?

The process whereby applicants for academic positions are selected sometimes seems haphazard, and sometimes it is, but I made an effort in this study to identify some general patterns. The material in this section is based

Figure 2. Institutional Movement of New College Teachers

☐ = Participants who went to a higher ranked department
▥ = Participants who went to a similarly ranked department
▨ = Participants who went to a lower ranked department

rank of department awarding Ph.D. (department and institution of first academic appointment)	Top 15 Departments	Departments Ranked 16-26	Unranked graduate departments	Institution with some grad. program	4-year Institution	2-year Institution	Institutions outside U.S.	TOTAL
1-7	2	5	10	3	3	0	2	25
8-15	6	4	10	4	2	1	4	31
16-26	1	6	8	10	1	0	3	29
unranked	0	0	8	2	1	0	1	12
TOTAL	9	15	36	19	7	1	10	97

Table 5. Location of Faculty Members by Type of Institution

	Study Population	All Geographers	All Full Time Faculty in the United States
Institutional Source of Support			
State	87%	74%	73%–Public
Local	1	6	
Private/Denominational	12	20	27–Private
Degree Given by Institution			
Many Graduate Degrees	66%	30%	38%
Some Graduate Degrees	24 } 33%	53	41
B.A./B.S.	9 }		
A.A.	1	16	20
Size of Institution (Enrollment)			
Less than 999	4%	5%	8%
1,000–4,999	11	21	27
5,000–9,999	18	24	21
10,000–19,999	24	24	21
20,000 +	44	25	23
Degrees Given by Department			
Ph.D.	40% } 62%	38%	—
M.A./M.S.	22 }		
B.A./B.S. Major	29	27	—
Less than B.A./B.S. Major	8	34	—
Size of Department (Number of Faculty Members)			
Less than 2	0%	14%	—
2–5	15	29	—
6–10	30	27	—
11–20	48	25	—
21 +	7	4	—

on responses from the chairperson and two other colleagues in the participant's new home departments.

Relative Importance of Teaching, Research, and Service. The first question was, How much relative importance did you yourself (that is, not the department as a whole or other members of the department) place on the conventional criteria of teaching, research, and service when you reviewed applicants for the position now held by the study participant? Table 6 shows the average relative weight (that is, the number of points out of 100) that these informants placed on such criteria.

When the data in Table 6 are compared vertically, the results are what I would expect. More value is placed on teaching ability in the smaller two- and four-year institutions than in the large graduate-oriented institutions, and the opposite is true for research. However, a horizontal comparison of the figures yields some surprises. Teaching was given more weight than research

Table 6. Relative Importance of Teaching, Research, and Service in New Academic Appointments

	Teaching	Research	Service	(N)
Type of Institution or Department (Source of Support)				
Local	77[a]	3	20	1
State	50	32	17	78
Denominational	61	20	19	5
Private	52	32	16	6
Type of Institution (Level of Program)				
2 year	77	3	20	1
4 year	60	22	18	9
Some Graduate Degrees	55	23	21	21
Major University	49	36	15	59
Type of Institution (Enrollment)				
Small (< 5,000)	63	17	19	17
Medium (5–13,000)	47	31	22	19
Large (13–26,000)	49	33	17	33
Extra Large (over 26,000)	46	39	13	22
Type Department (Level of Program)				
Less than B.A./B.S. Major	62	19	19	8
B.A./B.S.	56	23	20	27
M.A./M.S.	47	37	20	20
Ph.D.	47	40	13	34
Size of Department (Number of Faculty)				
Small (1–5)	61	20	18	13
Medium (6–10)	52	30	18	27
Large (11–15)	45	37	19	26
Extra Large (16 and over)	50	33	16	25

[a] Each figure represents the average rating given to that factor by the chairperson and two other colleagues in institutions or departments as indicated. Each set of figures sum to 100 horizontally. In some cases they do not total 100 exactly because of rounding.

in all categories of departments and institutions, even in the large graduate-oriented institutions. This finding counters all the images and impressions that people have of faculty appointments in graduate-oriented departments and institutions. What can account for this?

One possible explanation is that respondents say one thing on a questionnaire but make decisions otherwise. However, in a similar survey on the same question in a separate research project (Fink and Morgan, 1976), I tested this explanation by presenting respondents with five hypothetical candidates who varied in their teaching and research qualifications. The results of this test were consistent with the present data; namely, the candidate who is judged to have potential in both teaching and research is strongly preferred over the candidate who is a better researcher but a poorer teacher. Another possible explanation is that teaching qualifications are more important in obtaining an appointment but that research and publications are more important in acquiring tenure, promotions, and pay raises. Jacques Barzun, in the foreword of another study on this topic (Caplow and McGee, 1958, p. xi) has described "the radical ambiguity of a profession in which one is hired for one purpose, expected to carry out another, and prized for achieving a third: Teaching, research, and prestige are independent variables, besides being incommensurable per se."

However, another factor that turned up in this study — whether the new teacher has a tenure-track or a non–tenure-track position — sheds some light on this question. Fifty-five percent of the new teachers in our study received a non–tenure-track appointment. This figure changed from 40 percent in the first year of the study to 65 percent in the second year.

Figure 3. Criteria for Tenure-Track and Non-Tenure-Track Appointments

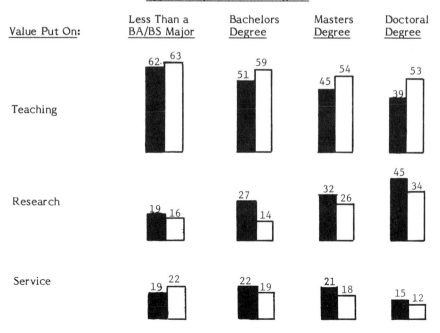

Departments that hire a new teacher on a non–tenure-track basis may place more value on teaching and less on potential for research than departments that hire on a tenure-track basis. The data shown in Figure 3 indicate that the type of appointment appears not to affect the criteria in departments with lower-level programs but that it does have a significant effect in departments with graduate programs. This seems to explain what is happening in Ph.D.-granting departments: In tenure-track positions, research is more important; in non–tenure-track positions, teaching is more important.

Other Criteria. What about other criteria than the three standard ones? The chairperson and colleagues were also asked whether six other characteristics were important to them in making their choice. These six characteristics and the percentage of respondents who indicated that the characteristic was important are as follows: Applicant has needed subject specialization (73 percent); applicant is congenial, has personal compatibility (60 percent); applicant is creative and innovative (33 percent); applicant is compatible with goals of institution (28 percent); applicant has capacity to teach a wide range of courses (26 percent); applicant is female or member of a minority group (5 percent). These data suggest that having the needed specialization and being able to get along with people are very important characteristics. Being creative and innovative is somewhat less important, but it is still helpful.

The chairpersons and their colleagues added a number of interesting comments to their answers. Several mentioned the fact that a candidate's availability at a late date was important. Here are two other telling comments:

"[The person was] raised in our area and is therefore less likely to leave after one year."

"ABDs (All-done-but-dissertation) come cheaper."

Types of Information Available. The final question about the selection process involves the information that colleagues had to help them decide who best fit their criteria. In this study, the participants' colleagues were asked to indicate which of eight types of information about the participants' teaching qualifications were available to them and whether this information was useful. The results are presented in Table 7.

Knowledge that the candidate had been a teaching assistant was the single most available and useful type of information. Its importance may have been related to the fact that almost half of the candidates had not given a visiting lecture in the department before they were appointed (item 3 in Table 7). The comments received relative to this question often referred to a letter of recommendation from a person whom the reviewer especially trusted. This study did not collect and analyze such letters, but a study by Lewis (1975) did. After reviewing more than 3,000 letters of recommendation, Lewis (1975, pp. 51–52) noted: "Information regarding teaching is often qualified with something on the order of 'I have no firsthand information, but I would guess

Table 7. Information Considered Valuable
in Making Academic Appointments

	Proportion of Colleagues for Whom the Information Was		
Types of Information	Available and Useful	Available but Not Useful	Not Available
Candidate has			
Experience as a teaching assistant	76%	8%	16%
Letter of recommendation from faculty member with expertise in geography and education	44	5	51
Given a visiting lecture	50	2	48
Completed a teaching practicum with feedback	25	3	72
Had seminar on teaching of geography in higher education	12	8	80
Written essay on his or her philosophy of teaching	9	2	89
Course evaluations of his or her teaching	9	3	88
Videotape of himself or herself teaching	0	0	100

from what I have seen (or heard) that...' Qualities most frequently mentioned are those that help to ensure good performance: fluency and enthusiasm. Attributes related to carrying out the task effectively—degree of organization and preparation, thoroughness and conscientiousness—are also emphasized... Seldom specified are interest in and dedication to the teaching enterprise in general."

Combined with the data from this study, Lewis's observations suggest that those who make decisions about academic appointments do not have much firsthand information about candidates (for example, videotapes, course evaluations, essays on teaching). Rather than collecting their own information and making their own evaluations, they rely on the judgment of others (that is, on the writers of letters of recommendation) who, if Lewis is right, have little firsthand information of their own. The resulting view of how judgments are made about the teaching qualifications of those who staff our colleges and universities is not reassuring.

Once the new teachers were on the job, several situational factors either helped or created major problems for them. This chapter describes these factors and their effects on the performance and professional satisfaction of the new teachers.

The Situational Factors Affecting Teaching

L. Dee Fink

Once the would-be professors had been offered a position and they agreed to accept it, a basic decision had been made. A critical stage of their academic career was about to begin. They had just received—or were still trying to finish the requirements for—the highest degree available in the American educational system. They had been examined—albeit hurriedly in some cases—and they had been offered a position of major responsibility in an institution of higher learning. After weighing the options—which for many were few at the time of this study—they had accepted responsibility for extending knowledge in their discipline and for teaching others.

This chapter presents information about what they found and what happened to them when they arrived in their new organizational home. It begins with a look at the type of contract that they had, at the status of their dissertation and at their teaching load. Then, it describes their relationships with the institution, with faculty colleagues, and with students. All these relationships profoundly affected the professional—and sometimes the personal—lives of the new college teachers in this study.

Type of Contract

During the period of this study, departments of geography were dramatically increasing the proportion of positions offered as non–tenure-track

L. D. Fink. *The First Year of College Teaching.* New Directions for Teaching and Learning, no. 17. San Francisco: Jossey-Bass, March 1984.

appointments. During the first year of the study, 1976, only 46 percent of the new positions accepted were non–tenure track. In the following year, the proportion was 63 percent. Some of these were one-year positions, and others were two-year.

We asked department chairpersons whether there was any possibility of converting non–tenure-track positions into tenure-track positions and if there was what determined whether it was done. To the question, Is there any possibility of retaining new teachers? 72 percent of the chairpersons answered yes. To the question, What factors are most important in the decision to retain? (respondents were allowed two choices), 64 percent of the chairpersons pointed to the new teacher's general performance, 56 percent to the new teacher's teaching ability, 23 percent to the status of the university budget next year, and 11 percent to increased departmental enrollment.

The reasons for the prevalence of non–tenure-track positions could be policies by college deans, late hiring, and departmental decisions to use non-tenure-track appointments as a way of checking on a new person's performance before a longer-term position is offered. The chairperson's responses lend support to the last explanation.

As Table 8 shows, the data from the study also indicate that people in non–tenure-track positions were evaluated slightly lower as teachers by colleagues and students, they found less intellectual companionship with colleagues, and they found less satisfaction in their first year as a teacher.

Status of Dissertation

Although disciplines vary in their willingness to accept new faculty members who have yet to finish their dissertations, two-thirds of the participants in this study started to teach before they had finished their dissertation. Thirty-four percent had completed their dissertation before they started teaching, 34 percent completed it during the first year of teaching, and 32 percent had not finished their dissertation by the end of their first year of teaching. Interviews with study participants indicated that having to work on the dissertation while teaching several courses, many for the first time, was a very difficult and time-consuming task and that it probably affected the quality of both activities.

Table 8. Performance and Satisfaction by Type of Contract

Type of Contract	Scale:	Colleagues' Evaluation 0–4	Students' Evaluation 1–100	Found Intellectual Companionship? 1 = no; 3 = yes	Found Satisfaction? 1 = no; 5 = yes
Tenure-track		3.3	35	2.2	4.0
Non–tenure-track		3.1	33	2.1	3.8

Size of Teaching Load

The appropriate teaching load for university faculty is hotly debated by faculty members, administrators, and even state legislators. Critics argue that professors should teach more, but professors respond that they are already teaching more than they should in order to do a good job. Unfortunately, these debates often overlook three important distinctions. The first has to do with the aspects of teaching load that create the work load effect of the assignment: the number of separate subject matter preparations required during the term, the number of students, the number of classroom hours per week, and the nature of the subject itself, since it sometimes involves much writing, lab work, and so forth. The second distinction relates to the nature of the institution. The major university, the university with some graduate departments, the four-year institution, and the two-year institution all vary in their expectations for research and publication as well as in their teaching assignments. The third distinction has to do with the level of teaching experience of individual faculty members. The professor who teaches a course for the first time requires much more preparation time than the professor who has taught it before, and new professors are teaching many of their courses for the first time. Furthermore, new professors are less efficient in finding and organizing new material than those who have taught several years. This study took all three distinctions into account. I made an effort to measure new professors' typical teaching loads in different types of institutions, to compare these loads with the loads of other faculty members, and to assess the effect of these teaching loads on teaching effectiveness and the sense of overload.

Typical Teaching Loads for New Faculty Members. Table 9 relates average number of classroom hours per week, class size, and number of separate subject matter preparations during the first year to type of institution. The average number of classroom hours per week varied quite sharply by institutional type, and it changed in the direction that one would expect. The number of separate preparations required of new teachers varied widely, especially in institutions with graduate programs. Nearly all participants in institutions devoted exclusively to undergraduate education had many subjects to teach in their first year. The most disturbing aspect of Table 9 in this respect is that more than 50 percent of the new college teachers in every type of institution had four or more separate courses to prepare and teach during their first year.

Class size did not vary significantly by type of institution. There was a wide range in class size over all four types of institution. The same pattern emerged when institutions were categorized by size of enrollment, as Table 10 shows.

The widespread belief that large institutions have a greater proportion of large classes than small institutions do appears to be without foundation, at

Table 9. Teaching Loads of Beginning College Teachers
by Type of Institution

		Average Number of Classroom Hours Per Week	
Number of Participants	Type of Institution	First Term	Second Term
63	Major University	6.7	7.0
23	Some Graduate Depts.	9.0	8.6
9	Four-Year Institution	8.7	8.3
1	Two-Year Institution	12.0	12.0

	Percentage of Participants Who Had Different Numbers of Separate Preparations During First Year					
Type of Institution	1	2	3	4	5	6–8
Major University	3%	10%	32%	33%	14%	6%
Some Graduate Depts.	4	4	35	35	9	13
Four-Year Institution	–	–	33	–	44	22
Two-Year Institution	–	–	–	–	–	100
Overall	3%	7%	32%	30%	15%	11%

	Percentage of All Classes That Were:			
Type of Institution	Small (1–14 students)	Medium (15–34)	Large (35–99)	Extra-large 100 +)
Major University	24%	38%	31%	7%
Some Graduate Depts.	28	35	33	4
Four-Year Institution	23	40	33	4
Two-Year Institution	17	33	50	–

least insofar as the teaching assignments of the new faculty members in this study are concerned.

Lighter Teaching Loads for New Faculty Members? Participants were asked to indicate whether they thought their teaching load was lighter, heavier, or about the same as the loads of colleagues. Table 11 displays their responses.

Only one in five of the new teachers in a major university thought that their teaching load was lighter than colleagues'. Approximately 40 percent of the new teachers in all institutions thought that their teaching load was heavier. If this perception is accurate, many departments would seem to be putting new teachers in a situation that aggravates the problems created by having to finish a dissertation, by their relative lack of teaching experience, and by having to teach many courses for the first time. If the perception is not accurate, departments have a communication problem that has implications for the morale of new faculty.

Table 10. Class Size by Type of Institution

		Class Size:			
Number of Participants	Size of Institution (Enrollment)	Small (1-14 students)	Medium (15-34)	Large (35-99)	Extra-large (100+)
28	Extra-large (25,000+)	25%	40%	30%	5%
25	Large (15-25,000)	20	38	35	7
29	Medium (5-15,000)	31	34	27	7
14	Small (less than 5,000)	22	33	42	3
96	Overall	24	35	31	6

Effects of Excessive Teaching Loads. This study examined new professors' teaching loads for their effect both on participants' teaching performance and on their sense of overload. Table 12 relates teaching load to new professors' performance.

The data in Table 12 indicate that, while the number of hours spent in the classroom each week does not have a large negative effect on course evaluation scores, the number of subject matter preparations and the size of classes do. (The differences for class size are in addition to the allowance made for class size in the IDEA course evaluation system.) Apparently, it is not the number of classroom hours itself that creates problems for new teachers but rather the number of class preparations and the number of students involved. This finding is significant in light of the figures noted earlier that more than 50 percent of all study participants had between four and eight separate subject

Table 11. Teaching Load by Type of Institution

	"How did your teaching load compare with that of the more experienced faculty members?"			
Number of Participants	Type of Institution	Heavier Load	Same Load	Lighter Load
56	Major University	38%	41%	22%
21	Some Graduate Depts.	43	57	0
8	Four-Year Institution	38	63	0
1	Two-Year Institution	0	100	0
	Overall	39%	48%	14%

Table 12. Effects of Teaching Load on Course Evaluation Scores

Number of Classroom Hours Per Week	Average Course Evaluation Score Scale: 1–100
1–4	28
5–7	34
8–10	36
11–13	31
14 +	28
Number of Concurrent Preparations During Term	
1	44
2	32
3	29
4	22
Size of Course Evaluated	
Small (1–14 students)	38
Medium (15–32 students)	35
Large (35–99 students)	30
Extra-Large (100 + students)	18

matter preparations during their first year (Table 9) and that 37 percent of their classes were large or extra large.

To what extent did large teaching loads, in conjunction with such other academic duties as advising students, supervising directed readings, writing research proposals, preparing articles for publication, and serving on committees create a sense of overload? When participants were asked whether they felt overloaded during their first year, 24 percent said that they did not feel overloaded. However, 69 percent said that they felt somewhat overloaded, and another 8 percent said that they felt totally overloaded. Respondents in the second group gave several reasons for their feelings. Forty-two percent of all respondents said that they gave first priority to their teaching and slighted other duties and needs as a result, while 15 percent of all respondents said that they slighted their teaching in order to attend to other duties.

What contributed most to new teachers' sense of overload? The contributing factor identified most frequently was a heavy teaching load, cited by 76 percent. Next was getting settled into a new community—44 percent; research—40 percent; student advising—35 percent; and committee work—20 percent. (The percentages sum to more than 100 because respondents were allowed to cite as many as three contributing factors.) Participants' comments often reflected their frustration. Here are three typical comments:

"Dissertation not worked on in fall term."

"Somewhat overloaded. My response: Division of time such that best job in each area of responsibility not achieved."

"I have been totally overloaded of my own volition in order to accelerate work on my dissertation."

Relating to the Institution

Although all roses may be the same in the minds of some poets ("A rose is a rose is a rose."), all institutions of higher education are not. Study participants were aware of some characteristics of their institution that affected both what they did as a teacher and their levels of professional satisfaction and performance.

Perceived Characteristics of Institutions. When participants were asked at the beginning of their first year whether they thought that their new institution was different from other institutions of higher education or unusual in some way, nearly half (41 percent) said that they did. Their reasons serve as a keen reminder of the variety of institutions that exist:

- Urban commuter college
- Politically conservative
- Broad liberal arts curriculum
- Emphasis on technical curriculum
- Emphasis on applied curriculum
- Small, old, wealthy, traditional
- Lots of freedom to innovate
- Catholic
- No traditional departments, only interdisciplinary programs
- High-caliber students
- Students with restricted backgrounds
- Proximity to Washington, D.C.
- Black college
- Christian, two-year college
- Excellent facilities
- Severe budget limitations
- Urban, inner city, associated with medical complex
- New institution with young faculty
- More hierarchical, authoritarian
- "As 'the' state university, it must be all things to all people."

Next, participants were asked whether they thought that these special characteristics affected them as teachers. Nearly a third (29 percent) said yes, but not all were sure how it would affect them. Their comments included the following:

- Must be adaptive (commuter institutions)
- Will use my freedom (lots of freedom to innovate)

- Affects students and the feedback I give them (Small, old, wealthy, traditional)
- Will require more preparation time (only interdisciplinary programs)
- Cannot assume anything (black college)
- Will be working with a predetermined curriculum (students with restricted backgrounds)
- Will be little chance for innovation (small, old, wealthy, traditional)
- Will require more preparation (high caliber students)
- Keep classes informal (new institution with young faculty)
- May need to get by without convenient materials (severe budget limitations).

Identification with the Institution. The site visit interviews first made me aware of an important factor that I eventually called *identification with the institution.* I made the first round of site interviews during October of the first year. During one of these visits, I asked an interviewee my common opening question, How are things going? He gave me a long look, then proceeded to tell me that he was just coming out of the depths of depression from his first few months at the institution. When I inquired further, he described himself as a casual, carefree undergraduate who later caught fire in a prestigious, small graduate school. He loved the feeling of free, vigorous research and inquiry. Then, he came to teach at this small, church-run undergraduate institution. Although the school placed no real constraints on him, he found the whole atmosphere of the school very different from what he had come to enjoy in graduate school.

This conversation led to a major "insight": When the new school is different from the graduate institution, dissonance is likely to occur. My next interview was at a small, private liberal arts college. There, I encountered a person who had done his degree work at a very well-known graduate department in a large state-supported university. Anticipating that this person must be having adjustment problems, I asked "Are you having any problems here?" His response surprised me. "No," he said, "I love it here." Inquiring further, I discovered that this person had made it through graduate school satisfactorily but that he had never felt at home there, not as he had at the place where he had been an undergraduate — a small private liberal arts college. Hence, I made a note to myself that I needed first to find out what kind of institution the new teacher identified with as a student, then to determine whether the present institution is similar to or different from it.

As a result of these experiences, I added a series of questions about institutional identification to the midyear questionnaire. I also asked study participants whether they thought that this factor affected their satisfaction, their performance, or both, and, if it did, whether the effect was positive or negative. The results are shown in Tables 13 and 14.

More than half of the study participants identified with the institution at which they did their doctoral work, while most of the remainder identified

Table 13. Identifying with the Institution:
Pattern and Effect on Satisfaction

Perceived Effect on Satisfaction

Institution identified with and present institution are:

Perceived Degree of Effect	Very Different	More Different Than Similar	More Similar Than Different	Very Similar	Total
Great	$21 \begin{smallmatrix} 6 = + \\ 15 = - \end{smallmatrix}$	$2 \begin{smallmatrix} 1 = + \\ 1 = - \end{smallmatrix}$	$4 \begin{smallmatrix} 3 = + \\ 1 = - \end{smallmatrix}$	0	27
Some	$15 \begin{smallmatrix} 0 = + \\ 14 = - \end{smallmatrix}$	$16 \begin{smallmatrix} 5 = + \\ 7 = - \end{smallmatrix}$	$9 \begin{smallmatrix} 3 = + \\ 6 = - \end{smallmatrix}$	$7 \begin{smallmatrix} 3 = + \\ 2 = - \end{smallmatrix}$	47
None	3	5	8	1	17
Total	$39 \begin{smallmatrix} 6 = + \\ 29 = - \end{smallmatrix}$	$23 \begin{smallmatrix} 6 = + \\ 8 = - \end{smallmatrix}$	$21 \begin{smallmatrix} 6 = + \\ 7 = - \end{smallmatrix}$	$8 \begin{smallmatrix} 3 = + \\ 2 = - \end{smallmatrix}$	$91 \begin{smallmatrix} 21 = + \\ 46 = - \end{smallmatrix}$

Note: + and − indicate the number of participants who thought this factor had a positive or negative effect on satisfaction.

with the institution at which they did their undergraduate work. One in seven did not identify with one institution more than with another.

It was clear that participants' satisfaction during their first year was affected by the degree of similarity between their present institution and the one with which they had identified as a student. More than 80 percent thought that it affected their satisfaction, and the direction of the effect was as one would expect: As the difference between the institutions increased, the perceived effect became increasingly negative.

When participants were asked whether the degree of similarity between their presnt institution and the one with which they had identified as a student also affected their performance as a teacher, more than 50 percent answered in the affirmative. Again, as the difference between the institutions increased, the perceived effect became increasingly negative.

These data enabled us to check the participants' perceptions against other indicators of their performance. Table 14 shows the average course evaluation score for the four categories of participants and similar figures for the assessments by chairpersons and by all three colleagues. In each case, the participants whose present institution was very different from the one with which they identified scored significantly lower than those whose present institution was similar.

Here are some comments that reflect the participants' perceptions and feelings. Said one participant whose present institution was very different:

Table 14. Identifying with the Institution: Effect on Performance

Perceived Effect on Performance

Institution identified with and present institution are:

Perceived Degree of Effect	Very Different	More Different Than Similar	More Similar Than Different	Very Similar	Total
Great	9 (4 = +, 5 = −)	3 (1 = +, 2 = −)	3 (2 = +, 1 = −)	0	15
Some	14 (1 = +, 10 = −)	8 (2 = +, 2 = −)	4 (3 = +, 1 = −)	5 (2 = +, 2 = −)	31
None	16	12	14	3	45
Total	39 (5 = +, 15 = −)	23 (3 = +, 4 = −)	21 (5 = +, 2 = −)	8 (2 = +, 2 = −)	91 (15 = +, 23 = −)

Three Indicators of Actual Teaching Performance

Average Course Evaluation Score[a]	26	32	39	40
Average Chairman Assessment[b]	2.6	3.3	2.7	3.2
Average Assessment of Three Colleagues[b]	2.7	3.0	2.9	3.1

[a] Scale: 1 (low) to 100 (high)
[b] Scale: 0 (low) to 4 (high)

"Shorter terms and greater course load mean it is not realistic to set high standards for students. The result is that course material covered each term is much less, and depth and extent of knowledge is less. . . . Students [here] often feel that 'anything that won't get me a job' is worthless. Yet, they have less of a 'professional' attitude toward their grasp of knowledge. . . more than at [the institution with which I iden-tified], the administration here seems to interfere or control teaching activities — format for syllabi, what courses can be offered in a depart-ment, and so forth."

"Found attitude here (and in field) toward recent Ph.D. graduates dehumanizing and too costly to continue to attract quality teachers to the field. Publication requirements here (and in the field) require emphasis on research (which I find easy) and not on teaching, which bothers me because I am unable to divorce myself from the career developments of students."

In a few cases, participants found the difference to be positive.

"I like the small college atmosphere and the rural environment. It is a change and—I feel—a positive one. You frequently meet your own students around the campus here. [At my other institutions], it was a rare occasion when you encountered one of your own students."

Institutional Support for Teaching and the New Teacher. One other important difference among institutions is the degree to which they provide support for teaching and for new teachers. For this reason, participants were asked whether they thought their institution's reward system encouraged high-quality teaching. In general, their responses followed the expected pattern: A larger proportion of participants in small undergraduate institutions thought that quality teaching was rewarded than participants in large graduate-oriented universities did, as Table 15 shows. It is disturbing that half of the new teachers thought that the reward system did not encourage good teaching or that they were not sure whether it did.

Participants' comments indicate that at least some of the institutional support for teaching was perceived as lip service:

Table 15. "Does the Reward System of Your Institution Encourage High Quality Teaching?"

(N)	Size of Institution	No	Don't Know	Yes	Yes & No
14	Small (< 5,000 enrollment)	7%	21%	57%	14%
29	Medium (5–15,000)	27	17	52	3
25	Large (15–25,000)	40	16	40	4
28	X-large (25,000 +)	39	18	43	0
	Level of Institutions				
1	2-Year	0%	100%	0%	0%
9	4-Year	11	11	68	11
23	Some Graduate Dept.	35	13	44	9
63	Major University	33	19	46	1
	Institutional Source of Support				
1	Local	0%	100%	0%	0%
83	State	36	15	46	3
5	Private	0	20	80	0
7	Denominational	0	43	43	14
96	Total	31%	18%	47%	4%

"No real knowledge, but although high-quality teaching is praised, it seems to have little to do with tenure decisions."

"It is, of course, encouraged but probably not rewarded."

"Everyone gets the same percentage raise if money is available. Promotion has nothing to do with pay. I'm not particularly uptight about promotion, tenure, and so forth. . . . Keep your nose clean and your ass out of hot water."

Finding Companionship with Colleagues

I discovered another situational factor, which I eventually called *intellectual companionship*, during one of my early site visits. I asked a new teacher in a medium-size university located in a small town how things were going, and he related the following story: He had been given an office on a different floor from the rest of the faculty. It was difficult to enter and leave the room without disturbing classes in session. Somehow, the secretaries repeatedly "forgot" to inform him of faculty meetings until they were over. His wife, who was waiting to see whether the job was permanent, had not yet joined him. Nevertheless, after two months, no one had invited him to dinner or to any other social occasion. He had to invite himself to professional events related to his own area of expertise. As a result, the person was feeling very isolated and alienated. He was disturbed about the situation, but he did not know what to do about it. After discovering that others faced similar situations, I asked all participants in the midyear questionnaire whether they had found intellectual companionship among their colleagues; that is, whether they had found colleagues with whom they could discuss ideas and professional concerns.

Effect on Satisfaction and Performance. Only one third of the participants had found such companionship. The remaining two thirds said either that they had not found it or that they had found it only to a limited extent. As Table 16 shows, the majority of this two thirds thought that it had had a negative effect on their professional satisfaction.

When asked whether this factor had affected their performance, two thirds said that it had. Their perceptions were supported by other indicators of teaching performance. Participants who had found intellectual companionship received significantly higher course evaluation scores from students and higher assessments from chairpersons and colleagues than participants who had not found such companionship, as Table 17 demonstrates.

Participants' comments shed some light on the reason why this factor was so significant. Here are some typical comments:

From Those Who Did Find Intellectual Companionship:

"The stimulation makes my work much more interesting. More interest and satisfaction makes it easier for me to perform."

Table 16. Intellectual Companionship:
Pattern and Perceived Effect on Satisfaction

Perceived Effect on Satisfaction

"Did you find intellectual companionship?"

Perceived Degree of Effect	No	Only to a Limited Extent	Yes	Total
Great	6 $\begin{smallmatrix}0 = +\\6 = -\end{smallmatrix}$	12 $\begin{smallmatrix}3 = +\\9 = -\end{smallmatrix}$	19 $\begin{smallmatrix}18 = +\\1 = -\end{smallmatrix}$	37
Some	9 $\begin{smallmatrix}2 = +\\6 = -\end{smallmatrix}$	30 $\begin{smallmatrix}10 = +\\16 = -\end{smallmatrix}$	9 $\begin{smallmatrix}8 = +\\1 = -\end{smallmatrix}$	48
None	1	6	3	10
	16 $\begin{smallmatrix}2 = +\\12 = -\end{smallmatrix}$	48 $\begin{smallmatrix}13 = +\\25 = -\end{smallmatrix}$	31 $\begin{smallmatrix}26 = +\\2 = -\end{smallmatrix}$	95 $\begin{smallmatrix}41 = +\\39 = -\end{smallmatrix}$

Note: + and − indicate the number of participants who thought this factor had a positive or negative effect on their satisfaction.

"I have begun to use educational games as a result of contact with a fellow teacher. I borrow slides and other visual aids from another instructor. My ideas are stimulated, and [they] develop through discussion with colleagues."

"Being able to talk to others at a satisfactory intellectual level makes a place more pleasant. This also helps clarify one's own thoughts, which makes it easier to present them to students."

From Those Who Found It Only to a Limited Extent:

"I greatly miss the daily interaction that I enjoyed as a graduate student. I am gradually building contacts, many of which are outside my department, to remedy this situation."

"Too darn little intellectual curiosity or excitement among the faculty in the department. I get more intellectual stimulus from the better students majoring in geography."

And from Those Who Did Not Find It:

"At times, I feel in a vacuum—alone. Most of our faculty seem to be pessimistic about almost everything—it rubs off on others (me). I probably spent 85 percent of the time last semester in a rather depressed and negative state of mind."

Table 17. Intellectual Companionship: Effect on Performance

Perceived Effect on Performance

"Did you find intellectual companionship?"

Perceived Degree of Effect	No	Only to a Limited Extent	Yes	Total
Great	$2 \begin{smallmatrix} 1 = + \\ 1 = - \end{smallmatrix}$	$3 \begin{smallmatrix} 2 = + \\ 1 = - \end{smallmatrix}$	$6 \begin{smallmatrix} 6 = + \\ 0 = - \end{smallmatrix}$	11
Some	$9 \begin{smallmatrix} 1 = + \\ 7 = - \end{smallmatrix}$	$24 \begin{smallmatrix} 11 = + \\ 10 = - \end{smallmatrix}$	$19 \begin{smallmatrix} 18 = + \\ 1 = - \end{smallmatrix}$	52
None	5	21	6	32
	$16 \begin{smallmatrix} 2 = + \\ 8 = - \end{smallmatrix}$	$48 \begin{smallmatrix} 13 = + \\ 11 = - \end{smallmatrix}$	$31 \begin{smallmatrix} 24 = + \\ 1 = - \end{smallmatrix}$	$95 \begin{smallmatrix} 39 = + \\ 20 = - \end{smallmatrix}$

Three Indicators of Actual Teaching Performance

Average Course Evaluation Score[a]	26	29	40
Average Assessment by Chairman[b]	2.7	2.7	3.3
Average Assessment of Three Colleagues[b]	2.6	2.7	3.2

[a] Scale: 1 (low) to 100 (high)
[b] Scale: 0 (low) to 4 (high)

"I feel socially and intellectually isolated. The lack of friends with whom I can discuss and develop ideas puts a damper on creativity. As a result, I have little interest in remaining in my present position over the long term."

Support from Colleagues. In addition to being intellectual companions, colleagues can do a number of things to help new teachers. A list of eight types of support that can be especially important for new teachers was presented to participants, who were asked how much of each type of support they had received from colleagues and whether they thought that more support would have been helpful. The colleagues of participants were also asked how much of each type of support they had provided to the new teachers.

One problem identified by this series of questions is a problem of perception: As Table 18 shows, for all eight types of support, participants thought that they had received less than colleagues thought that they had given. One possible explanation is that colleagues who have been in the organization for some time believe that such support is not very important or that, if it is, newcomers can get it on their own. However, the new teachers may feel a much stronger need for assistance, and they may not be at all sure how to get it.

When participants were asked whether they would have liked more support from colleagues, almost 80 percent checked one or more of the items listed in Table 18. For each type of support, except for invitations to professional events, between one fourth and one third of the new teachers would have appreciated more. One particularly disturbing aspect of Table 18 is that nearly half of the participants said that there had been little or no explanation of the local resources for teaching and that there had not been a careful explanation of the criteria by which their performance would be evaluated. Both kinds of support seem to be especially important for those who are beginning their careers as college teachers.

Table 18. Assessment of Colleague Support

Type of Support	New Teacher Ratings of "Support Received":			Average Rating, by All Colleagues, of "Support Given":
	Average	Percent Receiving "Little or None"	Percent Desiring More Support	
1. Invited participant to colleagues' classes	0.31[a]	93%	26%	0.54[a]
2. Offered to visit participant's classes	0.55	86	25	0.77
3. Discussed general teaching problems	1.47	50	26	2.48
4. Explained local resources	1.71	46	32	2.44
5. Carefully explained criteria for performance evaluation	1.72	46	26	2.17
6. Discussed particular courses and teaching at this institution	1.88	36	30	2.68
7. Invited participant to professional events	2.09	30	9	2.22
8. Invited participant to social events	2.34	29	23	2.36

[a] Scale: 0 (low) to 4 (high)

Participants' comments about support from their colleagues reveal how valuable the help was when it was given, how difficult life was when it was not, and how some felt guilty for not asking for it more aggressively:

"Things here are just as I would like."

"Very poor information on support-related material, services, and so forth."

"Perhaps I am too optimistic about the level of help that can be given to a new person, but I was lost and lonely for quite some time, both socially and academically."

"This was as much my fault as anyone else's. I could have asked more questions."

Classroom Observations. I also asked whether the new teachers had been able to visit the classes of colleagues to learn about teaching or whether colleagues had visited theirs. Interviews indicated such visits could have occurred as a result of team teaching, auditing of courses, sitting in on classes, and invitation.

The responses indicated that approximately 40 percent of the new teachers had been observed in the classroom by a colleague. Half of these observations were the result of team teaching situations. Of these respondents, very few said that they were excessively uncomfortable when they were being observed, and half said that they had learned something from their colleagues' suggestions that they had incorporated into their teaching. Moreover, 45 percent said that they had observed colleagues' classes, usually as a result of team teaching or of sitting in on a few classes. Again, more than half of those in this group said that they had observed things that they wanted either to incorporate into their own teaching or to avoid in their own teaching. These findings suggest that use of team teaching situations to ease new teachers into a full teaching load may be a good idea. The results would depend on the open-mindedness, maturity, and intellectual qualities of both parties.

Some comments reveal the kinds of things that participants learned when they were observed or when they observed others:

"Refrain from talking too fast."

"Techniques for generating discussion among small 'seminar' groups."

"Interacting with students more before class."

"The use of recent data and illustrations to lend credence to my arguments."

Observations of colleagues made participants want to avoid:

"Boring, unexciting lectures [delivered] in a disorganized manner."

"Verbal attacks on a student's intelligence when the student gives a wrong answer."

"Don't try to 'wing' it; go to class with definite objectives in mind."

Relating to Students

Of all the relationships in higher education, the most important is probably the relationship between the professor and his or her students. It is very complex, but it is also very critical for the performance and satisfaction of both parties to the educational endeavor. This relationship is the product of many day-to-day interactions. Although a survey study like this could not observe these interactions directly, it could and did assess some of the underlying factors that provide a context for these interactions. These factors create problems and opportunities for teachers in their efforts to build the kind of relationship that they want. This study analyzed the effects of two contextual factors: the participants' perceptions of student characteristics and the social similarity between teachers and students.

Perceptions of Student Characteristics. One of the early discoveries of participants was that the students at various institutions are not all the same. When participants were asked whether they thought that the students at their new institution were different from most other college students, almost half answered in the affirmative. Here are some comments that describe traits that they saw and their responses as teachers:

> "Affluent! Generally intellectually motivated, sound academic background. [Response:] Use discussions to bring out issues, perspectives; work for student–student interaction as well as student–teacher interaction."

> "Most are fully employed outside school. [Response:] Reduce outside-of-class required work."

> "Not as mature or conceptually sound as students at my graduate institution. [Response:] Will emphasize applied aspects of geography."

> "They are black, come from poor educational (and home) environments—poorly prepared in reading-writing-verbal skills. [Response:] Go back to the basics and cover material in a much slower, more explanatory fashion."

After being asked to describe their students' general characteristics, participants were asked to assess their students' readiness for college-level work. Participants described their perceptions both at the beginning of the year and at midyear. Table 19 presents the results.

At the beginning of the year, more than 80 percent of the participants thought that the descriptions in Table 19 were true or at least moderately true

Table 19. Teachers' Perceptions of Students' Readiness for College-Level Work

Students in This Institution:	Perceptions at Beginning of Year				Mid-Year Changes in Perception		
	True	Moderately True	Not True	(Not Significant)	Worse	Same	Better
1. Have an adequate academic foundation for college work, that is							
a. Have a high level of substantive knowledge	19%	56%	22%	(3%)	38%	52%	10%
b. Can read effectively	30	45	12	(14)	29	66	5
c. Can write effectively	14	51	25	(11)	52	41	7
2. Readily accept their academic responsibilities (attend classes, do assigned readings, and so on)	52	36	5	(6)	24	64	13
3. Accept the importance of learning	38	48	7	(7)	13	76	12
4. Are motivated (eager to learn)	34	49	3	(2)	19	64	17
5. Understand what they should learn in a class without being told	21	53	21	(5)	35	59	6
6. Are capable of abstract, formal thinking	19	56	21	(4)	38	52	11
7. Can integrate what they learn in class into their personal and professional thinking	33	47	12	(8)	12	75	13

of most students. However, the perceptions of between one fourth and one half of the teachers had changed, mostly for the worse, by midyear. The biggest drops occurred in their perceptions of students' writing ability, students' abstract thinking ability, students' background knowledge, and students' ability to understand what they should learn in class without being told.

This situation has the potential for creating conflict over academic standards. That it did create problems was revealed by participants' responses to two questions. In response to the question, Is there a significant difference between the prevailing academic standards for students at this institution and your own standards? 70 percent answered yes, while only 30 percent answered no. Those who indicated that there were significant differences were then asked, What has been your response? One percent said that they had raised their standards, 51 percent that they had maintained their standards, and 47 percent that they had lowered their standards. The participants' disillusionment with their students' academic readiness and their felt need to compromise their own academic standards suggest that there were fairly widespread problems in the relationship between new teachers and students. The educational background and attitude of students, the expectations of teachers, and the ability of new teachers to relate to and motivate their students were presumably all contributing factors. The next section describes another factor specifically related to the ability of new teachers to communicate with and motivate their students.

Social Similarity of Teachers and Their Students. During one of the early site visits, I visited a new teacher who had been raised in a large city in one region of the country and who had a particular religious background. Now, he was teaching rural and small-town students from a different region of the country who had a different religious background. I saw a major communication problem when I visited that teacher's class. Each party was making verbal and nonverbal statements that the other party either missed or misinterpreted. Subsequently, I discovered that other participants had difficulty relating to students with different social or cultural backgrounds. Consequently, I asked participants on the end-of-year questionnaire to identify themselves and the majority of their students in terms of seven social characteristics: economic status (income level), urban or rural background, regional origin, national origin, religious orientation, race, and age.

Extent of Differences. Most of the new teachers described themselves as white, protestant, middle-income Americans. They varied in age, regional origin, and urban or rural background. Students had the same general characteristics, except for age, and there were fewer agnostics. However, the new teachers were often working in institutions where students were different from themselves. Table 20 shows that the greatest number of teachers differed from students in terms of regional origin, urban or rural background, religion, and — as one might expect — age.

Effect on Performance. Relatively few new teachers thought that these social differences were having a negative influence on their teaching (Table 20).

Table 20. Teacher-Student Similarity and Perceived Effect

Social Characteristic	Percent of Teachers Who Were		Total Number Who Thought the Effect of this Factor on Their Teaching Was:			
	Different	Similar	Negative	Neutral	Positive	(Uncertain)
1. Region of Origin	62%	38%	24 $\begin{array}{l}22=D\\2=S\end{array}$	30	30 $\begin{array}{l}16=D\\14=S\end{array}$	13
1. Rural-Urban Background	62	38	14 $\begin{array}{l}12=D\\2=S\end{array}$	44	27 $\begin{array}{l}12=D\\14=S\end{array}$	12
2. Religious Orientation	60	40	7 $\begin{array}{l}6=D\\1=S\end{array}$	69	2 $\begin{array}{l}2=D\\0=S\end{array}$	19
4. Age	96	4	14 $\begin{array}{l}14=D\\0=S\end{array}$	45	19 $\begin{array}{l}15=D\\3=S\end{array}$	19
5. Economic Background	19	81	4 $\begin{array}{l}3=D\\1=S\end{array}$	52	24 $\begin{array}{l}1=D\\23=S\end{array}$	17
6. National Origin	12	88	3 $\begin{array}{l}3=D\\0=S\end{array}$	67	15 $\begin{array}{l}3=D\\12=S\end{array}$	12
7. Race	9	91	2 $\begin{array}{l}1=D\\1=S\end{array}$	66	13 $\begin{array}{l}2=D\\11=S\end{array}$	16

Note: D and S indicate the number of participants who were "different from" or "similar to" their students.

Only one fourth thought that different regional origin, urban or rural background, and age created problems. However, as Table 21 shows, when the teaching evaluations were examined, the teachers who were similar to students in every social characteristic except age received better student evaluations and equal or better colleague evaluations than teachers who were not.

The performance indicators for age differences are mixed. However, for this characteristic, we might expect a reverse effect: Teachers who are close in age to their students may find it easier to understand students, but they may also find it more difficult to establish their professional authority.

Table 21. Three Performance Indicators on Dimensions of Teacher-Student Similarity

Social Characteristics	Average Student Evaluation Score[a]	Average Chairman Assessment[b]	Average of Three Colleague Assessment[b]	(N)
1. *Economic Background*				
(Teacher and students were:)				
Similar	33	2.9	2.9	78
Different	28	2.9	2.9	17
2. *Urban-Rural Background*				
Similar	35	3.0	2.9	36
Different	31	2.8	2.9	59
3. *Region of Origin*				
Similar	33	3.3[3]	3.1[2]	36
Different	32	2.7	2.7	59
4. *Religious Orientation*				
Similar	35	3.0	3.0	39
Different	30	2.8	2.8	56
5. *Race*				
Similar	34[2]	2.9	2.0[2]	86
Different	17	2.4	2.4	9
6. *National Origin*				
Similar	33	3.0	2.9[1]	84
Different	26	2.1	2.5	11
7. *Age*				
Similar	30	3.3	3.5[1]	4
Different	32	2.9	2.8	91

[a]Scale: 1 (low) − 100 (high) (IDEA Evaluation Instrument)
[b]Scale: 0 (low) − 4 (high)

Note: The difference between the means is significant at the following levels:
[1]$p < 0.10$
[2]$p < 0.05$
[3]$p < 0.01$

Cumulative Effect. The next question is whether the effect of these social differences is cumulative. That is, did teachers who were relatively similar to their students do better than teachers who were relatively different? Clearly, the answer is yes. As Table 22 shows, as the number of social similarities between teacher and student increases, so do the average teaching evaluation scores from colleagues and from students.

Many comments from participants shed light on how the students' social characteristics worked for them or against them. Some participants described other social differences that, while less tangible, were equally significant:

"Always hard to come from one region and acquire proficiency in the trends and attitudes of another. Age has been a bit of a problem in that I'm not much older than my students—and look it! Religion is not really a problem, except that [the dominant church here] is very conservative on many conservation-related issues, like resource exploitation and family planning."

"I came from a wide-ranging background, and therefore, I find it easy to understand students and put them at ease in a formal educational framework."

"The effete Eastern snob in me may have occasionally rubbed some students the wrong way initially, but this was usually smoothed over within a short time. The black-white thing was no real problem."

"The National Origin dimension worked both negatively (in terms of my understanding of the students) and positively (in terms of their willingness and desire to interact with me)."

Table 22. Effect of Teacher-Student Similarity on Teaching Effectiveness

Number of Dimensions of Teacher-Student Similarity	Average Student Evaluation Score[a]	Average Chairman Assessment[b]	Average of Three-Colleague Assessment[b]	Number of Participants
6 (Very Similar)	46	3.5	3.3	4
5	36	3.3	3.2	21
4	33	3.0	2.9	36
3	31	2.5	2.6	21
2	24	2.4	2.5	8
1 (Very Different)	18	3.0	2.9	4

[a]Scale: 1 (low) to 100 (high)
[b]Scale: 0 (low) to 4 (high)
Note: The dimensions of teacher-student similarity did not include age as a factor.

"I see myself as a product of the pre-TV/mass media/entertainment culture [where it was thought that] 'work may be hard.' The students are products of mass media/entertainment cultures [where it is thought that] 'all learning must be entertaining.'"

Summary

This chapter has reviewed information about the situation that the new teachers encountered when they arrived in their new organizational home. Much of this information is not reassuring. Before they even began, 55 percent were placed in a position of uncertainty and tenuousness by being given only a temporary, non–tenure track appointment. Two thirds still had not finished their dissertation by the time they started teaching. This increased the impact of the heavy teaching load that most received. Nonetheless, half managed to finish their dissertation during the first year.

The new teachers' teaching load varied significantly with the type of institution. New teachers in major universities averaged only six classroom contact hours per week, while those in four-year institutions and two-year institutions averaged nine and twelve hours respectively. More than half (56 percent) had courses that involved four or more separate subject matter preparations during the first year. This makes it easy to understand why new teachers seldom had time to think about and experiment with different teaching techniques or to undertake work on their own development as a teacher. The data also indicate that as the number of course preparations and the size of their classes increase, the course evaluations that new teachers receive from students decrease. The vast majority of participants in this study felt overloaded and attributed this feeling primarily to an excessive teaching load.

The institutions in which the new teachers worked also exerted a major effect. Participants were conscious of many distinctive characteristics, and they made some effort to adjust to the different demands and challenges of each. But, the majority also found that their new institution was different from the one with which they identified as a student, and when they were asked whether this affected their performance and the satisfaction that they derived from their work, they replied that it did. This perception was supported by the course evaluation scores given to the new teachers by students and by the assessment of colleagues. New teachers who worked in an institution that was similar to the one with which they identified as a student were rated as more effective than new teachers who worked in an institution that was not. Finally, fewer than half were sure that the reward structure of their institution encouraged high-quality teaching. This perception affected their relationship with their new institution.

A second type of relationship was the type developed with the participants' colleagues. One problem in this case was that the majority of the teachers did not find much intellectual companionship, that is, someone with whom they could share professional ideas and concerns. Again, they thought this adversely affected their satisfaction with the job and performance. Course evaluations and colleague assessments supported this view. Those who found such companionship were rated by both students and colleagues as more effective teachers than those who did not. The new teachers also indicated a desire for more of several types of support. There seemed to be a problem in the professional support given to the new teachers by their colleagues. The ones who did receive it (for example, an invitation to observe other teachers and/or to be observed), found it helpful.

Finally, some information was learned about the new teachers' relationships with their students. Many participants were surprised by their students' lack of academic readiness. The problem of communication barriers between the new teachers and their students compounded this. The task of exciting students, humoring them, exhorting them, challenging them, disciplining them, and leading them intellectually requires a keen sense of how students think, feel, and react. This sense seemed to be reduced when the teachers had different social backgrounds than the students. Some were able to transcend these differences and quickly learned how to relate effectively to new students from different backgrounds than themselves. In a few cases, teachers were able to transform their differences into advantages. But most teachers did not adapt quickly to this factor and, in general, the more different a teacher was from his or her students, the lower was his or her rated effectiveness.

The new teachers revealed a certain level of idealism and some conservatism in what they tried to accomplish as teachers. Their ability to achieve their educational goals was limited and varied from class to class.

How the New Teachers Performed

L. Dee Fink

One fact became quite clear during this study: Teaching was the dominant activity for nearly all new professors during the first year. The task of preparing for and teaching their courses consumed the vast majority of their working hours. As this chapter will show, the degree to which they experienced personal and professional satisfaction during the first year depended to a great extent on how they fared in the classroom. Thus, this study asked four questions about their performance as teachers: What were the new professors trying to accomplish as teachers? What teaching methods and strategies did they use? How well did they do? How did they feel at the end of the first year about their experience as a college teacher?

What Were They Trying to Accomplish?

A set of values, beliefs, and images lies behind every decision that one makes as a teacher. Our beliefs about what good teaching is and our images of the teaching that exemplifies this ideal guide our decisions about a course and our actions in the classroom. Hence, it was important in this study to investigate the new teachers' values concerning what should happen and their beliefs about what would happen in the classroom. These subjective factors significantly influence the participants' ultimate satisfaction or dissatisfaction with their own teaching as well as what actually happened in the classroom.

Their Educational Goals. To get a clearer sense of the participants'

L. D. Fink. *The First Year of College Teaching.* New Directions for Teaching and Learning, no. 17. San Francisco: Jossey-Bass, March 1984.

fundamental goals and values, I asked them at the beginning of the year to complete a sentence beginning, "The most important thing I can do for students is." Of course, their responses were very different, but analysis of their comments revealed five lines of thinking. These lines of thinking are listed and illustrated with participants' comments in Figure 4. These statements are fairly illustrative of the range of ideals to which new college teachers aspire. The new teachers were often attracted to two or more of the goals just listed, as their comments often show.

Figure 4. New Teachers' Educational Goals

To Promote General Intellectual Growth	"provide the opportunity to develop analytic thinking."
	"help them to become 'intelligent skeptics.'"
	"provide them with the opportunity to grow as individuals."
To Teach Mastery of the Subject Matter or the Discipline	"instruct them in the fundamental principles and techniques of the particular subject under study."
	"give them the ability to analyze a situation from a geographic or spatial viewpoint."
	"help them to become thinking and able geographers."
To Develop Application Skills for a Vocation or for Living	"help them to learn and apply what they have learned."
	"make them aware of a body of knowledge or a set of techniques that increases their information base and that is useful to them in a practical sense."
	"help them to apply what they have learned to everyday life."
To Engage or Develop Students' Feelings	"enhance students' sensitivity to their surroundings. I want them to be turned on like I was turned on; I want to create 'gleams in their eyes.'"
	"convey the excitement that can be gotten from the pursuit of knowledge for its own sake."
	"teach and advise and stimulate students so that they can enjoy the learning of new ideas as an education and reward in itself."
To Prepare Students for Further Learning	"If I can stimulate their interest and provide them with some basic guidelines for learning, they will take care of the matter of educating themselves in terms of a longer process than my one-semester course."
	"facilitate an enjoyable learning experience that will place them in a position to learn more on their own at a later date."
	"instruct them in such a way that, upon completion of the course, they are and will continue to be able to assess, analyze, and interpret their environment."

However, all goals were not mentioned an equal number of times. Indeed, when participants' responses were analyzed and coded for the type of goals to which they made reference, I found that promoting general intellectual growth was mentioned fifty-three times, teaching mastery of subject matter and discipline was mentioned thirty-six times, developing application skills was mentioned twenty-five times, engaging students' feelings was mentioned twenty-three times, and preparing students for further learning was mentioned twenty-one times.

What do these statements and frequencies reflect? To begin with, they reflect high ideals. The majority of the new teachers were trying not just to teach a specific course or subject matter but to achieve some greater good, some general intellectual growth or to lay the groundwork for future learning. One fourth of the participants directed their statements to the intermediate goal of exciting students and engaging their feelings, although some probably viewed this as a valuable goal in and of itself. Many of the statements referring to application skills seemed to reflect the applied ethos of the institution in which the participant was now teaching.

Did these goal statements represent something more than noble but empty rhetoric? Did they actually guide the teaching efforts of these new faculty members? It is not possible to answer this question conclusively without more information on the interaction between teacher and students than I was able to obtain, but it is possible to get a partial answer by looking at the course objectives selected by teachers for the IDEA evaluation process. Were the objectives that participants selected for their courses consistent with their general goal statements?

As Table 23 shows, the course objectives were generally consistent, but some expected differences did not show up. For example, those who wanted to promote general intellectual growth indicated that learning to apply course

**Table 23. Course Objectives Selected by Teachers
with Different Goals and Values**

	IDEA Course Objectives Selected:	
Goal Statements	More Frequently	Less Frequently
Promote general intellectual growth	Thinking and problem solving Creative capacities	
Teach subject matter mastery		Creative capacities
Develop application skills		Factual knowledge General liberal education
Engage students' feeling	Personal responsibility	Principles and theories Effective communication
Prepare students' for further learning		

material to improve rational thinking, problem solving, and decision making was an important course objective more frequently than the other teachers did. In contrast, neither the objective of developing the skills and competencies needed by professionals in this field nor the objective of learning how professionals gain new knowledge were selected any more often by those who said that they wanted to develop students' application skills than they were by others.

Another type of evidence suggests that the new teacher encountered problems in translating their ideas into appropriate kinds of teaching activities. The IDEA questionnaire asks students to rate the frequency with which a teacher used each of twenty teaching methods or activities. These methods and activities are then sorted into four different groups—one related to involving students, one to communicating content and purpose, one to creating enthusiasm, and one to preparing examinations. We might expect that new teachers who wanted to teach subject matter mastery would rate higher on communicating content and purpose than teachers who did not espouse this goal. But, most of the relationships that we might expect did not show up. Only two categories of goal statement showed significantly higher ratings on the measures of teaching activities: Those who wanted to promote general intellectual growth were rated significantly higher on involving students in the course, and those who wanted to prepare students for further learning were rated significantly higher on creating enthusiasm.

Their View of Self as a Teacher. The teacher is the second major factor in the teaching equation. What self-images guided the activities of these new teachers? Axelrod (1973) has described four different teaching prototypes that he believes exist in the profession of college teaching. These prototypes are the images that each teacher has of the kind of teaching that he or she believes to be most worthwhile; that is, they are the teacher's vision of the teacher at his or her best. Participants were given a brief description of Axelrod's four teaching prototypes; then, they were asked to rank order the four images in terms of their own preference.

As Table 24 shows, their responses reveal a fairly orthodox approach to teaching. The majority said that they preferred what Axelrod called the principles-and-facts prototype. Apparently, they felt most secure with this approach. Although Axelrod believed that teachers can change prototypes in any sequence, his description of the evolution of a hypothetical teacher's changing view of teaching begins with the principles-and-facts prototype. This study suggests that he was right in so doing, since this seems to be the most common prototype among new teachers. Since they probably do not yet feel sufficiently confident as scholars or teachers to teach what they are, they emphasize what they know.

Mann and his colleagues (Mann and others, 1970) elaborated six different roles that a teacher can fulfill or avoid fulfilling when relating to students — expert, formal authority, socializing agent, facilitator, ego ideal, and person.

Table 24. Role of Self in Teaching for New Teachers

	Choice:	
Their Preferred Teaching Prototype (after J. Axelrod)	First	First or Second
Principles-and-facts ("I teach what I know.")	52%	78%
Instructor-centered ("I teach what I am.")	20	44
Student-as-mind ("I train minds.")	22	56
Student-as-person ("I work with students as people.")	7	23

	Role Fulfillment (after R. Mann)		
Role	Desired	Perceived	Difference
Expert	3.65[a]	3.44[a]	– 0.21
Formal authority	2.52	2.64	+ 0.12
Socializing agent	2.38	2.07	– 0.31
Facilitator	3.10	2.52	– 0.58
Ego Ideal	3.20	2.58	– 0.62
Person	3.07	2.95	– 0.12

[a]Scale: 1 (low) to 4 (high)

Role	Function
Expert	Transmits the information, concepts, and perspectives of the field.
Formal Authority	Establishes rules, sets procedures, and selects goals.
Socializing Agent	Introduces students to the values, assumptions, and life-style of the profession and clarifies goals and career paths beyond the course.
Facilitator	Searches for ways to help students learn and grow within their own frame of reference and helps to overcome obstacles to learning.
Ego Ideal	Conveys the excitement and value of intellectual inquiry in a given field of study.
Person	Presents himself or herself as and recognizes the students as persons, thereby validating the full range of human needs and human experiences.

The new teachers were asked both the degree to which they wanted to fulfill each role and the degree to which they thought they were perceived by students as fulfilling each role. Table 24 shows the desired level of role fulfillment, the perceived level of role fulfillment, and the difference between the two for the study population as a whole. Participants were most attracted to the role of expert, which is consistent with their prototype preference. Ego ideal was the second most desired role, which seems consistent with the comments that many had made about identifying with the discipline of geography. In general, participants thought that students saw them as fulfilling these roles less than they wanted to themselves, except for the role of formal authority. Apparently, they felt that students were more apt to place them in the role of taskmaster than they themselves wanted to be.

Their Views of the Knowledge Necessary for Teaching. One questionnaire asked the new teachers whether they thought that the kind of knowledge required for research was similar to or different from the kind of knowledge required for teaching. This issue has been debated in higher education for some time. Earl McGrath (1950, p. 34), commissioner of education under the Eisenhower administration, has long argued that research and teaching call for very different kinds of knowledge, skills, and competencies:

> "The research worker, concerned with the minute analysis of an ever narrower area of reality, requires a knowledge of research techniques and skill in their use. The prospective teacher, on the other hand, though he should have an imaginative and vital mind and the capacity for critical analysis, must master wide ranges of subject matter, learn the habit of philosophic synthesis, and acquire certain pedagogical skills and professional attitudes."

Recently, Cahn (1978) offered a new version of this thesis. Arguing against the view that the publish-or-perish syndrome is responsible for poor undergraduate teaching, Cahn believes that publishing should help, not hinder, good teaching. In his opinion, the real problem is a "failure to recognize the crucial principle that intellectual competence and pedogogic competence are two very different qualities" (Cahn, 1978, p. ix).

In response to the question, Is the kind of knowledge required to do research on a topic similar to or different from the kind of knowledge required to teach the same subject? 19 percent of the participants in our study said that it was very similar, 44 percent said that it was more similar than it was different, 25 percent said that it was more different than it was similar, and 12 percent said that it was very different. This means that nearly two thirds (63 percent) of the respondents shared the view that dominates the ethos of graduate schools; namely, that the two kinds of knowledge are more similar than they are different.

Origins of Their Views. Although the responses of participants were diverse, most participants were fairly conservative in their educational values and beliefs. They preferred the principles-and-facts prototype, they were most attracted to the role of expert, and they believed that the knowledge necessary for teaching was basically similar to the knowledge required for research. Where did these values and beliefs come from? What were some of the major influences in their formation?

One of the first questionnaires asked the new teachers about the origin of their approach to teaching. Forty-one percent said that it was modelled primarily on one or two teachers; 39 percent said that it was eclectic—that is, borrowed equally from many teachers; 18 percent said that it was independent—that is, that it had been created without much modelling; while 3 percent said is was some combination of the preceding. This pattern underscores the major influence of prior teachers, either of one or two who were especially admired or of several whose influence was felt in combination. Only a small minority said that they were trying to create their own independent approach to teaching.

Another question of special interest in this study was whether participation in one of the TLGG programs described in Chapter One seemed to influence the participants' values and beliefs. Table 25 depicts the educational values and beliefs of three subgroups of the study population: those who did not participate in a teaching preparation program during graduate school, those who participated in a teaching preparation program but did not value it, and those who both participated in and valued such a program.

Table 25. Effects of Participating in a Teaching Preparation Program on Educational Values

Participants Who—		TLGG Participants	
	Non-Participants	Not Valued	Valued
A. *Made goal statements about:*			
Mastery of subject matter	48%	29%	6%
General intellectual growth	48	64	75
Engaging students' feelings	30	7	25
Preparing students for further learning	19	36	25
Developing application skills	23	21	38
B. *Valued the following teaching prototype:*			
"Principles-and-facts"	81%	86%	60%
"Instructor-centered"	43	50	40
"Student-as-mind"	60	28	66
"Student-as-person"	17	36	33
C. *Desired the teaching role of:*			
Expert	97%	92%	93%
Formal authority	56	62	38
Socializing agent	56	31	31
Facilitator	75	62	75
Ego ideal	77	69	94
Person	79	85	68
D. *Believed that:*			
Knowledge for teaching and for research are more different than similar	36%	15%	56%

Although there were some differences between program participants and nonparticipants, most of the major differences seemed to be between participants who valued the TLGG experience and those who did not. Most of those who valued the TLGG experience expressed values that were more liberal and less conventional than the statements both of TLGG participants who did not value the program and of nonparticipants. Those who valued the TLGG program were low on the mastery of subject matter goal, on the principles-and-facts teaching prototype, and on the formal authority role. They were high on the goal of general intellectual growth, on the student-as-mind teaching prototype, on the ego-ideal role, and on seeing the knowledge necessary for teaching and research as different in nature. This finding clarifies the question of what happened in these programs. The programs themselves were based on certain educational values. Participants who found these values acceptable responded positively to the program and seemed to benefit from it. Participants who did not accept these values did not value the program and did not benefit from it.

What Teaching Methods and Strategies Did They Use?

Having determined what the new teachers wanted to accomplish educationally, the next logical question was: What did they do to achieve these goals? My ability to answer this question was perhaps the least satisfactory part of this research project. A survey study based primarily on questionnaires is not well equipped to determine the way in which new teachers do such things as design their courses, gather illustrative examples for a lecture, or develop class exercises, all of which have a major effect on the quality of a course. The only thing that I was able to do was to ask whether the new teachers intended to use certain teaching techniques and strategies and whether they did anything to improve themselves as a teacher.

Use of Specific Teaching Techniques. At the beginning of the year, participants were asked what teaching techniques they intended to use. However, the comments of many respondents made it clear that the way in which they had to teach was often not the way in which they wanted to teach. Several factors forced them out of their preferred mode of teaching:

"Due to size of classes, lack of TAs, and lack of time, I'll be working mostly from a lecture format this year."

"Often, I would like to use an activity, but it is not realistically feasible; for example, field trips and PSI (Personalized System of Instruction) (can't work this up in one quarter)."

"I use slides and overhead transparencies almost every day in one course or another. Unfortunately, the classroom and personnel organization here [large state university] are less conducive to teaching methods than the community college where I taught formerly."

Given the constraints of time, class size, and facilities, what techniques, then, did the new teachers use? Essentially, they all used lectures and readings (Table 26). Most used audiovisual aids and some form of class discussion. Several used library research projects. Only a few used other methods of teaching. The main reason why more new teachers did not use a wider range of techniques was undoubtedly the lack of time and perhaps their lack of familiarity with other teaching techniques. Recalling the information presented in Table 9 in the preceding chapter — more than 55 percent of the new teachers had four to eight separate new courses to prepare during their first year — it is not surprising that most resorted to the lecture-and-readings approach that requires relatively less advance preparation and organization time.

Alternative Teaching Strategies. I made an effort to determine whether participants had automatically started to teach in a particular way or whether they had considered a number of alternatives, then made a reasoned choice. Hence, participants were asked at the beginning of the year whether they had given serious consideration to more than one form of teaching, and, if they had, what forms they had considered and later rejected.

This question elicited a large number of extended comments, which suggests that the new teachers had given a lot of thought to the subject. Several new teachers had wanted to hold seminar-like discussions, but they found it necessary to reject this form of teaching because of large enrollments. Others found themselves changing their teaching approach in response to student characteristics. One respondent said,

Table 26. Teaching Techniques Used

	Percentage of Respondents Who Used This Technique in:		
	Three or More Classes	Only One to Two Classes	Zero Classes
Lectures	78%	22%	0%
Readings (text, library materials)	77	22	1
Audio-visual aids	66	24	10
Discussions of particular readings	53	37	10
General class discussions	48	39	13
Library research project	25	48	27
Field trips	12	37	51
Laboratory work	12	37	51
Field-based research project	11	47	42
Simulation games	7	42	51
Computer-based instruction	6	26	68
Audio-visual tutorial	2	4	94
Personalized system of instruction (PSI)	1	6	93

"I'm using less formal lecture in the World Regional course and more of it in the Anglo-American course. [This is] is response to the alertness, responsiveness, and so forth of the [two] classes."

Other responsdents gave more tentative replies, indicating they were still experimenting and feeling their way along:

"I am still considering the possibilities of increased emphasis on field work in several classes. Changes depend on how much time I have to explore and develop local potential."

Efforts to Improve Themselves as Teachers. All teachers, new or experienced, need to work to improve themselves. To what degree were participants in this study doing this? On the midyear questionnaire, they were asked: What activities have you engaged in during the past half year that were specifically intended to improve your competence as a teacher? Their responses to this and related questions are displayed in Table 27. About one fourth said that they engaged in activities specifically intended to improve their competence as a teacher. Several more said that some incidental experiences had helped them as teachers.

Next, participants were asked what they had done to improve their teaching ability. The responses fell into one or more of three categories.

Improved my knowledge of the subject I teach (N = 21)

"Read a great deal to improve my substantive knowledge."

"Audited a team-taught course on environmental studies."

"Attended a week-long seminar at Purdue University on remote sensing."

Table 27. Efforts by New Teachers to Improve Their Teaching

	Yes	*No*
"Did you engage in any activities specifically intended to improve your competence as a teacher?"	27%	73%
"Were there incidental activities that helped you as a teacher?"	38	62
"Did you modify your teaching as a result of what you learned?"		
Greatly	6	—
To a limited extent	74	—
Not at all	20	—
"Did you utilize local teaching support services?"	63	37

Studied some aspect(s) of college teaching (N = 16)

"Read books relating to interpersonal communication."

"Attended a series of miniworkshops within the college on 'The Improvement of Teaching.'"

"Read articles on college teaching."

Familiarized myself with the locale and local resources (N = 6)

"Traveled to get slides and experiences to make class more interesting."

"Attended workshop on AV-aids in teaching."

It was not surprising to see new teachers trying to improve their knowledge of the subjects that they had been asked to teach. It was surprising to hear that 16 percent had actively sought out knowledge about college teaching. Nevertheless, one in six is still a small proportion. Half of the members of this group were taking advantage of some type of workshop offered by their institution or at professional conferences. The other half were doing something on their own.

How Well Did They Teach?

The simple-sounding question, How well did they teach? is in fact very difficult to answer. The difficulty arises from the fact that three other questions have to be answered first. One of the embedded questions is, How well did they teach—according to whom? The students? The teachers themselves? Their colleagues? An outside observer? The second embedded question is, In what sense did they teach well? Did they give good lectures? Did they lead good discussions? Did they get their students excited? Did they grade their students fairly? Did they achieve their learning objectives? The third question relates to different kinds of teaching situations: Did they teach well (or poorly) in all courses, or did their performance vary significantly in different kinds of teaching situations? If their performance varied, was there a common kind of situation in which the majority did well or poorly, or was there not? This study took all three of these embedded questions into account.

Sources of Information. Information about the teaching performance of the new teachers was gathered systematically from three primary sources: the teachers themselves, their colleagues, and their students. In addition, as director of the study, I visited the classrooms of thirty participants, where I obtained some general impressions.

These sources were not all equally well informed. I was the least well informed, because I saw only one class session for only some participants. In contrast, the students were present at a significant number of sessions for one course for each teacher. The teachers themselves attended all or nearly all sessions of all the courses that they taught. The degree to which their colleagues were well informed is not totally clear.

The questionnaire for colleagues asked them to identify the information on which they based their assessment. As Table 28 shows, most seemed to base their evaluations on conversations with the new teacher, with students, or with both. For the most part, their evaluations were not based on personal observations of the new teacher in the classroom. It was somewhat surprising that nearly 50 percent of the colleagues other than chairpersons said that they had seen course evaluation results. Nevertheless, there is reason to be somewhat cautious about the frequencies reported by colleagues for these activities. Although twenty-nine chairpersons said that they had visited participants' classes one or more times, only twenty-one participants reported being visited by anyone. Thus, some responses may indicate what colleagues intended to do or what they thought they should have done. The net result is that colleagues had various sources of information, almost all of which were indirect. The adequacy of these sources is an open question.

Types of Information. The second complicating factor concerns the multidimensional character of teaching. Teaching involves and requires many

Table 28. Colleagues' Sources of Information About the Teaching of the Study Participants

	Chair	Colleague Number 1	Colleague Number 2
1. No Information on Participant	1%	8%	39%
2. Visited Participant's classes			
• Percent "not at all"	68%	72%	74%
• Average frequency	0.8[a]	0.7	0.5
3. Talked with Participant about his/her classes			
• Percent "not at all"	9%	14%	11%
• Average frequency	2.4	2.3	2.4
4. Saw the results of their course evaluation			
• Percent "not at all"	26%	49%	51%
• Average frequency	2.4	1.5	1.4
5. Heard reports from students in their classes			
• Percent "not at all"	11%	9%	8%
• Average frequency	2.0	2.3	2.4
6. Comments by other faculty			
• Percent "not at all"	15%	24%	30%
• Average frequency	2.0	1.7	1.6
7. *Completeness* of the information you have			
• Percent "no information"	0%	2%	3%
• Average rating	2.5[a]	2.4	2.2

[a]The "average frequency" is based on a scale ranging from 0 (none) to 4 (quite a lot). The "average rating" (item 7) is based on a scale ranging from 0 (no information) to 4 (very complete).

different skills and competencies. The many evaluation instruments developed over the years each have their own list of important aspects of teaching. Four lists were used for our study. One was created specifically for our study, and three were borrowed.

A list of six common teaching functions was developed for the study. New teachers were asked to evaluate themselves as a lecturer, as a discussion leader, as a test maker, as a student adviser, as a person interacting with students, and as a creative teacher. A list developed by Hildebrand and others (1971) consists of five general academic qualifications that were found to be important when faculty members evaluate one another: research competence, intellectual breadth, activity in the academic community, relation with students, and concern for teaching. This list was used with new teachers and with colleagues. Next, a list developed by Fink and Morgan (1976) contains eleven characteristics. It comes from a study of factors that are important when a department makes new academic appointments. This list was used with new teachers and with colleagues. The fourth source of information was the IDEA course evaluation system developed at Kansas State University by Donald Hoyt (Hoyt and Cashin, 1977). This is a sophisticated instrument that, for this study, obtained students' reactions to twenty teaching behaviors, students' perceived achievement on ten possible course objectives, summary scores for four general types of teaching behaviors, students' responses to four questions specific to this study, and an overall evaluation based on achievement of faculty-chosen course objectives as compared with other professors using IDEA in courses similar in terms of class size and student motivation.

The many questions on these four lists were analyzed for the types of information that they provided about the new teachers' qualifications and performance. The analysis resulted in a finite and structured list of aspects of teaching that this study undertook to evaluate:

A. *General Considerations*
   1. Teacher's knowledge of the subject
   2. Teacher's attitude toward teaching
   3. Teacher's ability to design courses
   4. Teacher's desire to continue learning about teaching
B. *Particular Abilities* ("Is the teacher able to...")
   1. Make course objectives clear
   2. Establish good relationships with the students
   3. Involve students
   4. Effectively communicate the course content
   5. Use particular techniques effectively (e.g. lecturing)
   6. Create enthusiasm
   7. Provide frequent and useful feedback to the students
   8. Change the teaching approach as appropriate
   9. Provide intellectual leadership
   10. Construct good tests

C. *Overall Assessment*
   1. As perceived by the teachers themselves
   2. As perceived by their colleagues
   3. As perceived by their students

Thus, the study asked one or more questions about each aspect of teaching, and each question was often asked of two or three audiences. The only aspect that was not covered well in this study was item A3, teacher's ability to design courses. In my mind, this refers to the teacher's ability to develop a uniquely organized set of learning activities that takes into consideration the particular curriculum, the subject, the students, the teacher, and the constraints in any given teaching-learning situation. To measure this in the survey study format, I settled for using a question from the study by Fink and Morgan (1976): "[The participant] has a well-developed philosophy of teaching and learning."

General Analysis of Participants' Teaching Performance. The actual evaluation data are presented in Table 29. In this section, I will identify and

**Table 29. Evaluations of the Teaching Performance of
Beginning College Teachers**

	Mean Rating Given by:		
Aspects of Teaching	*Teachers*	*Colleagues*	*Students*
A. *General Considerations*			
1. *Teacher's knowledge of the subject*			
• "Research activity and recognition"	2.70	2.93	-
• "Intellectual breadth"	2.62	2.90	-
• "Knows the subject matter of the course well"	3.10	3.39	-
2. *Teacher's attitude towards teaching*			
• "Concerns for teaching"	2.81	3.15	-
3. *Teacher's ability to design courses*			
• "Has a well-developed philosophy of teaching and learning"	3.56	2.86	-
4. *Teacher's desire to continue learning about teaching*			
• "Is interested in self-evaluation and continued development as a teacher"	3.16	3.30	-
B. *Particular Teaching Abilities*			
1. *Makes course objectives clear*			
• "Makes well-considered course objectives clear to students"	2.64	2.87	-
• "Clearly stated the objectives of the course"	-	-	2.72
2. *Establishes good relationships with the students*			
• "Able to interact with students in class" (first of year)	3.11	-	-

Note: All means are on a scale of 0 (low) to 4 (high) unless designated otherwise by the following code:
   a = 0 (low) to 2 (high)
   b = 1 (low) to 4 (high)
   c = 1 (low) to 100 (high)(50 = average for all teachers using IDEA system with similar courses)

Aspects of Teaching	Mean Rating Given by:		
	Teachers	Colleagues	Students
• "Clearly stated the objectives of the course"	-	-	2.72
2. *Establishes good relationships with the students*			
• "Able to interact with students in class" (first of year)	3.11	-	-
• (Mid-year change in perception of) "ability to interact with students in class" (0 = not as well as expected; 2 = better than expected)	1.22[a]	-	-
• "Relations with students"	3.23	3.32	-
• "Shows concern for students as individuals"	3.19	3.32	-
3. *Involves students in class*			
• "Teacher valued active student participation in this course"	-	-	1.59[a]
• "Involving students" (average summary percentile from IDEA for six questions related to this factor)	-	-	32[c]
4. *Effectively communicates course content*			
• "Communicating content and purpose" (average summary percentile from IDEA for six questions related to this factor)	-	-	47[c]
5. *Uses particular teaching techniques effectively*			
• (Self-rating as a) lecturer. (First of year)	2.84	-	-
• (Mid-year change in self-rating as a) lecturer (0 = not as well as expected; 2 = better than expected)	1.13[a]	-	-
• "Gives well-organized lectures"	2.86	2.91	-
• "Spoke with expressiveness and variety in tone of voice"	-	-	2.56
• (Self-rating as a) discussion leader. (First of year)	2.56	-	-
• (Mid-year change in self-rating as a) discussion leader (0 = not as well as expected; 2 = better than expected)	0.98[a]	-	-
6. *Creates enthusiasm*			
• "Is dynamic and enthusiastic as a teacher"	2.88	3.10	-
• "Seemed enthusiastic about the subject matter."	-	-	3.24
• "Stimulated students to intellectual effort beyond that required in most courses"	-	-	1.87
• "By the end of the course, have you (the student) come to see the subject matter as something important and meaningful to you?"	-	-	3.07[b]
• "Creating enthusiasm" (average summary percentile from IDEA for five questions related to this topic)	-	-	42[c]

Table 29. Evaluations of the Teaching Performance of
Beginning College Teachers *(continued)*

	Mean Rating Given by:		
Aspects of Teaching	*Teachers*	*Colleagues*	*Students*
7. *Provides feedback to students*			
• "Teacher provided frequent and helpful feedback on your performance as a student"	-	-	2.80[b]
8. *Changes teaching approach as appropriate*			
• "Uses a variety of teaching formats (computer-assisted instruction, field teaching, gaming, and so on)"	2.11	2.74	-
• "Changed approaches to meet new situations"	-	-	2.17
9. *Provides intellectual leadership*			
• "Challenges students intellectually"	2.78	3.16	-
• "Presents alternative perspectives of the subject matter"	2.64	-	-
10. *Constructs good tests*			
• (Self-rating as) a test maker. (First of year)	2.63	-	-
• (Mid-year change in self-rating as) a test maker (0 = not as well as expected; 2 = better than expected)	1.14[a]	-	-
• "Evaluates students for more than memorization of material from lectures and the test"	3.00	3.17	-
• "Preparing examinations" (average summary percentile from IDEA for three questions related to this factor)	-	-	52[c]
C. *Overall Evaluation*			
• "Did your general teaching strategy work better than, or not as well as, you expected?" (asked at mid-year) (0 = not as well; 2 = better)	0.78[a]	-	-
• "How does this teacher's performance compare to that of other beginning college teachers you have known? (0 = bottom 10%; 4 = top 10%)	-	2.87	-
• "Would this teacher's teaching performance be an asset or a liability for re-appointment or promotion?" (0 = definite liability; 4 = strong asset)	-	3.19	-
• "Overall evaluation (average summary percentile from IDEA, based on student perception of achievement of teacher's course objectives)(50 = average for all teachers with similar courses)	-	-	32[c]

discuss the items that were especially high or low for the whole group. Next, I will compare the ratings made by the three different evaluators—students, teachers, and colleagues. Finally, I will examine the general pattern of the new teachers' performance.

Best Aspects of Their Performance. In general, the new teachers were rated high on four items: establishing good relationships with students (B2), knowledge of the subject matter of their courses (A1), interest in self-evaluation as a teacher (A4), and evaluating students for more than memorization (B10).

Most of these findings are not too surprising. The fact that the new teachers were relatively young seems to explain their ability to relate well to students. The fact that they had just finished graduate school probably accounts for their own and for colleagues' perceptions that they knew the subject matter of the courses that they taught. However, this assessment did not extend to other types of knowledge: Colleague ratings of the intellectual breadth of the new teachers was much lower. The participants' high interest in self-evaluation and continued development as a teacher suggests that they were aware both of their own limitations and of their need for greater maturity as teachers. As test makers, the teachers rated themselves and they were rated by students as average, except for their ability to ask questions that required more than recall of material from lectures and text for which they received a high rating. Most of the specific IDEA questions about preparing examinations resulted in average scores, but on the question that asked whether the teacher's exams stressed things other than memorization, the new teachers received a high score.

Worst Aspects of Their Performance. There were five areas in which the new teachers received relatively low ratings: stimulating students to high intellectual effort (B6), changing teaching approach as appropriate (B8), involving students in class (B3), leading discussions (B5), and having a well-developed philosophy of teaching and learning (A3).

The single lowest score received by the new teachers collectively on their IDEA course evaluations was for stimulating students to intellectual effort beyond that required in most courses. Although this is identified in Table 29 as a question relating to creating enthusiasm (B6), it is also clear that it pertains to providing intellectual leadership (B9). There are probably two problems here. One lies in knowing how much work to demand of students. It is obvious that new teachers are at a disadvantage in this regard. The other problem lies in knowing how to stimulate (that is, how to motivate) students to do the work that is necessary in order to learn. The good relationship that the new teachers had with students did not suffice to motivate students to high intellectual effort. Apparently, motivation requires other abilities that the new teachers as a group did not possess to a high degree.

The fact that students rated the new teachers low on their ability to change their teaching approach to meet new situations (B8) is probably due to their lack of familiarity with more than one or two approaches to the teaching of a given topic or subject and to the limited time that they had in which to develop additional approaches. It takes time to think up different approaches, to try them out, and to refine them. Because of their heavy teaching load, the new teachers did not have this time.

As for involving students in class (B3), the students thought that the new teachers valued active student participation, but they did not think that the teachers succeeded in eliciting it. Given that the teachers themselves valued the principles-and-facts teaching ideal and the role of expert more than they valued the role of facilitator (Table 24), it is surprising that students thought that the new teachers valued student participation. In my opinion, the fact that the new teachers did not succeed in involving students relates to their ability to lead discussions. During my site visits, many of the new teachers whom I interviewed expressed frustration at their own inability to generate a good class discussion. After trying a few times without success, several new teachers gave up and switched to straight lecture. At the beginning of the year, the new teachers rated themselves on several dimensions. The second lowest rating that they gave to themselves was on their ability to lead discussions (B5). This perception had not changed by midyear. The fact that they felt more confident in their lecturing ability (B5) than in their discussion-leading ability at the outset and that they felt even stronger about this by midyear probably explains why many made the shift in teaching techniques that was reported in the interviews.

The last item with a relatively low rating was having a well-developed philosophy of teaching and learning (A3). This low rating is presumably a result of the failure of most graduate programs to encourage graduate students to develop such a philosophy and of the fact that the majority of the participants had little or no independent teaching experience or education course work.

The Three Sources of Evaluation Compared. When the ratings made by the three different evaluators—teachers, colleagues and students—are compared, some interesting patterns emerge. In almost all cases where the new teachers and their colleagues were asked the same question, the new teachers rated themselves lower than their colleagues did. The new teachers may have been measuring themselves against their own ideals and self-expectations, whereas their colleagues may have been comparing them with other new teachers or even with themselves when they first began teaching. Whatever the reason, the judgments of the colleagues were in general less harsh than those of the new teachers.

The student ratings varied. On some items, the students gave the new teachers higher ratings than the new teachers gave themselves; on other items, the ratings were lower. For example, on a scale of 0–4, students' mean rating on the item *Teacher was enthusiastic* was 3.24, while the new teachers' self-rating on the same item was 2.88. On the item *Teacher explained course objectives clearly,* the students' rating was 2.72, while the new teachers' self-rating was 2.64. On three items—*Challenged students intellectually, Ability as a discussion leader,* and *Ability as a lecturer*—the ratings that students gave were lower than those of the teachers: 1.87 versus 2.78, 2.19 versus 2.65, and 2.72 versus 2.86 respectively.

General Pattern of Their Performance. Part C of Table 29 displays the overall or general evaluation given by each of the three evaluators. Each group of respondents gave different responses, but in part the differences reflect the different kinds of summative questions posed to each group.

The teachers themselves were asked at midyear whether their general teaching strategy had worked as well as they had expected. Thirty-four percent said that it had not worked as well as expected, 53 percent said that it had worked about as well as expected, and 13 percent said that it had worked better than expected. The negative interpretation of these figures is that the number of new teachers who fell short of their own expectations was considerably larger than the number of those who exceeded their expectations. The positive view is that two thirds of the new teachers did as well as or better than they had expected.

The colleagues were asked to evaluate the performance of the new teachers in two ways: as compared with other beginning teachers whom they had known and as compared with the performance expectations for reappointment and promotion. The overall response to both questions was generally positive, although it was slightly higher for the second question. A halo effect seemed to be operating: Seventy-five percent of the participants were rated above average when compared with other new teachers, and thirty-three percent were said to be in the top 10 percent. (Grade inflation seems to be everywhere.)

The overall evaluation of new teachers by students, using the IDEA system, basically indicated whether students thought that they were learning what the teacher was trying to teach. Using national norms broken down by similarity of class size and student motivation, the new teachers as a group scored 32 on a percentile scale of 100. This means that their average score was better than 32 percent of the other teachers who used the IDEA system with similar courses. This is about one standard deviation below average. A decile-by-decile comparison of evaluation scores for the new teachers with scores for all teachers using the IDEA system shows a distribution for the new teachers that is overrepresented in the lower half of the scale (Fig. 5).

T scores were also calculated for each participant in the study using the IDEA system data base supplied by the Center for Faculty Evaluation and Development in Higher Education at Kansas State University. *T* scores come closer to providing a measure of absolute differences than percentile scores do. Then, the number of new teachers who had *T* scores more than one-half standard deviation higher or lower than the average for all teachers was calculated. For 31 percent of the new teachers, the *T* score was more than one-half standard deviation below the average for all teachers. For 57 percent, it was about average (that is, plus or minus one-half standard deviation), while for 13 per-

Figure 5. Profile of Course Evaluation Scores

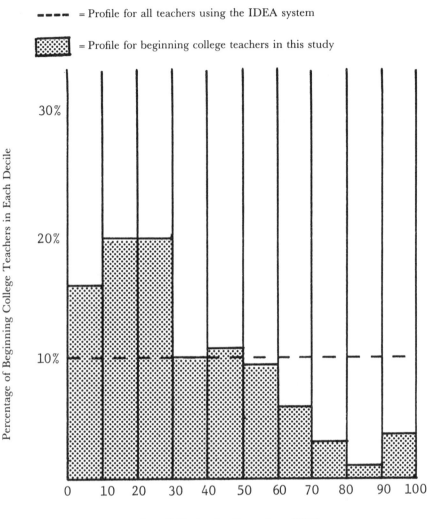

Overall Evaluation Score from IDEA

cent it was more than one-half standard deviation above the average for all teachers. This suggests that one in six of new college teachers will do an excellent job even in their first year, about half will perform on a level comparable to other more experienced teachers, and one in three will have significant problems.

Observations from Site Visits. As already mentioned, I made a series of one-day site visits to a third of the study participants that allowed me to interview them and sit in on one of their classes. These visits did not allow me to make a well-based general evaluation, but they did allow me to make some interesting observations, especially when they were related to the student and colleague evaluations that came in later. I will describe and comment on three of these observations here.

One interesting way in which the study participants differed involved their relative ability to read the pedagogical situation quickly and accurately. That is, some participants quickly recognized significant characteristics of their teaching situation that affected the way in which they designed their courses and taught. For example, one participant noticed that both the students and the institution were highly structured. Other participants responded to such things as the vocational orientation and the high or low intellectual level of their students and of the institution. Many of the characteristics that participants were quick to assess were the characteristics assessed in this study; some participants went even further in their analysis. However, the important point is that some participants not only recognized these characteristics very quickly, but they were also able to identify and make an appropriate educational response.

A second noticeable difference among the participants involved their ability to establish rapport with the students. Like the variable just mentioned, this ability is rather intangible. However, it was very clear when I walked into some classes that the teacher had developed a dynamic relationship with the students. That is, the teacher had the students' attention, and the students were making an effort to learn. It was also clear that this ability was something very different from merely entertaining or pampering the students. In classes where rapport had not been established, the students and the teacher both acted as if it was going to be a long semester.

The third interesting difference involved the new teachers' approach to teaching. Most new teachers seemed to be having better success with traditional forms of teaching, such as lectures leavened with some questions, than with less conventional forms of teaching, such as the project method and discussion-based inquiry. However, two qualifications need to be made. First, a few participants were trying unusual forms of teaching, such as simulation exercises, with much success. Second, while those who were experimenting with less traditional forms of teaching may not have done as well during their first year as the others did, they at least had an opportunity to broaden their knowledge of alternative ways of teaching and of what it takes to make these approaches work well. For example, one participant tried the project approach during the first semester, and it did not work well. However, he identified some ways of improving it and tried it again in the second semester, and it worked much better. It may be that new teachers must decide whether it is important to do well their first year, or whether they can afford to experiment with and learn how to use a variety of teaching techniques effectively.

Variations in the Quality of Teaching. One other question that is important to ask when evaluating teachers is whether the quality of their teaching is consistent from one course to another or whether it varies to a significant extent. This question is especially important to ask with beginning teachers.

At least one course was evaluated for every study participant, but forty-six participants also agreed to use the IDEA system in two or more classes. This provided an excellent opportunity to see whether the quality of teaching for these new teachers was generally stable or highly variable. The resulting multiple evaluations involved either multiple sections of the same course during the same term, of the same course during different terms, or of different courses. Thirty-four participants used the IDEA system two times, and twelve used it three, four, or five times.

The actual evaluation scores for all forty-six new teachers are shown in Figure 6. The scores shown are the summary evaluation percentiles. For

Figure 6. Professors with Multiple Course Evaluation Scores

Course evaluation scores for each professor:

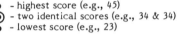

- highest score (e.g., 45)
- two identical scores (e.g., 34 & 34)
- lowest score (e.g., 23)

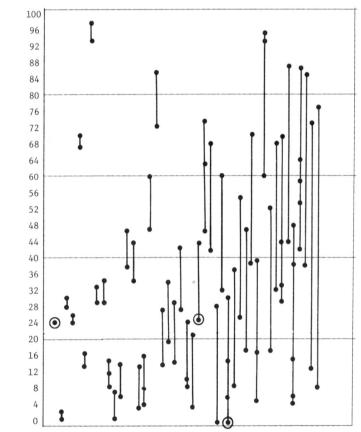

Each vertical line shows the scores for one professor.

several participants there was a large range between their highest and lowest scores. Figure 7 arranges the same set of scores in order of increasing range for individual professors. The range extends from 0 to 69. The horizontal dashed line in Figure 7 at the level of 22 is equal to one standard deviation for the course evaluation scores of all study participants. It represents the standard amount of variation between teachers. Twenty-one (46 percent) of the forty-six teachers who had multiple evaluation scores had an individual range of scores greater than 22. This means that, for nearly half of the new teachers, the variation between their highest and lowest scores (that is, the intrapersonal variation) was greater than the standard deviation in the scores of all new teachers in the study (that is, the interpersonal variation). This finding suggests that the course evaluation scores of beginning college teachers are highly variable.

What can account for this variability? One possible explanation is that

Figure 7. Range in Multiple Course Evaluation Scores

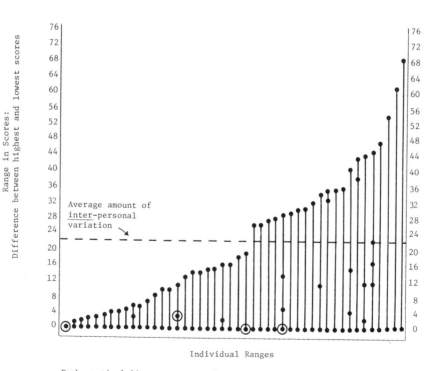

Each vertical line represents the range in scores for a professor with two or more course evaluation scores.

the IDEA instrument is not reliable. I reject this explanation for two reasons. First, the instrument has been tested for reliability by its creators. For classes in which at least twenty-five students provided ratings, the estimated reliabilities averaged .87, with a standard error of measurement of 0.3 (Hoyt and Cashin, 1977). Second, where I already had information predicting that a second course evaluation score would drop, the drop occurred. In one case, the participant went from teaching a course with which he was familiar and in which he was interested to teaching a course for which his levels of knowledge and interest were very low. In another case, the participant became embroiled during the second term in political turmoil within a small department. In both cases, the second round of evaluation scores was much lower. My conclusion is that the IDEA instrument is quite reliable, but the phenomenon being measured—the quality of teaching done by new teachers—is not stable.

Next, I made an effort to identify known factors that could account for this high degree of intrapersonal variation in course evaluation scores. None of the following factors regularly accounted for this variation: familiarity with or interest in the subject matter, time of year (fall or spring term), or the hour at which the course was scheduled. Hence, although these contextual factors presumably affect individual cases, other factors have a more significant and regular effect on the quality of the teaching. One possibility involves the relationship between the new teacher's personality and the collective "personality" of the new teacher's students. Another possibility is that new teachers find it difficult to deal with changing factors, known or unknown; hence, their teaching effectiveness varies substantially from course to course.

How Did They React to Their Experiences as College Teachers?

The experiences of the first year had a major impact on the attitudes of new teachers toward higher education, toward the profession of college teaching, toward other college professors, and even toward themselves. Information about their reactions came from their responses to an open-ended "miscellaneous comments" question in the midyear questionnaire and from their responses to three questions on the end-of-year questionnaire.

Feelings at Midyear. The last question in the midyear questionnaire, which most respondents completed in January or February, asked, Have there been any noteworthy events in your first half year not mentioned above that affected you as a teacher? Often, such open-ended questions will not elicit much response in a survey questionnaire, especially if the questionnaire is ten pages long, as it was in this case. Nevertheless, this question prompted an outpouring of comments, which I took to be an indication of the emotional sig.nifiicance of the new teachers' early experiences.

The midyear comments contained a number of themes. Several of these themes recurred in the end-of-year questionnaire, but the comments were not always made by the same people. The comments that follow, which are not arranged in any particular sequence, reflect the more prominent themes that emerged at this time.

(Isolation) "It can get fairly lonely here at times. My contact with the other faculty has been minimal. Really, the students are the only 'socially significant others' that I have."

(Disappointment with students): "I was disappointed with the outcome of last semester's evaluation results. I feel I've identified some points that needed improving—keeping in closer touch with students and so forth—but I'm very disappointed in the apparent total lack of regard (and knowledge) among the students of issues (for example, environment, politics, social problems). Most of the students come from middle- and upper-income families in [a suburban metropolitan area], and the lack of enthusiasm and participation is surprising."

(Exhaustion) "Took a one-year leave of absence from here to doctoral program. . . grant just sufficient to prevent absolute poverty. . . eroded savings account. . . moved back. . . bought a house. . . finished writing dissertation. . . had a son (first child) in October. . . taught a full teaching load (twenty contact hours per week). . . in December returned to graduate school to defend, correct, print dissertation, plus three-week consulting contract. . . returned here for eleven graduate course lecture hours per week. . . general exhaustion. . . postgraduate depression and generally wondering if teaching enthusiasm is gone."

(Insecurity) "The administration has devised a contingency plan in the case of drastic economic cutbacks. Among other things, tenured faculty can be released. It makes me wonder if I will put in my hours of study, years of economic sacrifice, and years of personal sacrifice just to eventually wind up being released and having to earn a living in some job that requires little or no college education. I don't lose sleep over the prospect, but it does make me doubt the worth of staying up until 10:30 every night writing lectures."

Feelings at the End of the Year. One question on the end-of-year questionnaire, which most participants completed in May or June, was this:

"There seems to be significant variation in the degree to which an individual's first year of teaching provides 'psychic satisfaction', that is, positive gut-level feelings about his/her experience as a teacher. To what degree have your experiences as a teacher this past year produced psychic satisfaction for you?"

This distribution of responses is shown in Table 30. In general, two thirds of the respondents had basically positive feelings, one in ten had negative feelings,

Table 30. Amount of Satisfaction from the First Year's Experience

Very satisfying	21%	**64%**
Moderately satisfying	43%	
No strong feelings one way or the other	5%	**24%**
Very mixed feelings	19%	
Rating unsatisfying	8%	**11%**
Very unsatisfying	3%	

and two in ten had very mixed feelings. Almost half of the respondents chose to make narrative comments amplifying their answer to this question. Most of the comments were made by participants whose feelings were negative or mixed, but several were made by participants whose reaction was positive. The themes and quotes that follow illustrate the range of comments.

Feelings were very different in different courses (N = 8):

"I had a great sense of satisfaction and a broadening of my knowledge and abilities in the seminar with a small number of highly motivated students. In the large lecture courses, it was highly rewarding to 'see the lightbulbs go on,' but so many of the students were just marking time and unwilling to be challenged."

"I would like to be teaching only in my field: geography. That will come in several years. I enjoy teaching anthropology and archaeology. I dislike teaching sociology; I'm not a sociologist, and it takes too much preparation time."

Enjoyed teaching but not other aspects of academia (N = 3):

"Very mixed feelings overall. Towards my students and classes, I am very satisfied. However, I feel this university is run like Penn Central."

"Classroom time is very satisfying, but otherwise rather unsatisfactory. It depends on whether you wish to disaggregate teaching (time in classroom, office hours, and so forth) from the rest of the 'crapola' that goes on at both the department and college level."

Feelings varied greatly from day to day (N = 3):

"Very mixed feelings. Teaching is a real emotional seesaw. I feel I do very well one day and very poorly the next."

"Some moments are very satisfying. Others are not. Overall, they tend to balance, although the satisfying ones are diminishing."

Satisfaction reduced due to overload and time constraints (N = 7):

"Everything is done is such a rush that I feel incompetent much of the time. I do a good job with the time I have but a mediocre job in absolute terms."

"I wish I had more time for preparation and a smaller teaching load. The experience might have been very satisfying."

Disappointed in experience (N = 8):

"I feel I have produced an excellent lecture series in each course and spent all my time to help students, create good tests, and so forth without any emotionally positive return. I have been insulted, cheated on and lied to by the students, and misled by my supervisors and the administrators."

"Very disappointed in my effectiveness as a teacher (as recognized by my students). I sense that questionnaire results do not reflect what is actually going on in the classes."

Sense of having improved (N = 4):

"There is always a question mark in grad school if you're getting into something you may not be satisfied with or qualified for, but after a shaky beginning, I feel I have progressed well, and the students have learned something about cultural and urban geography from taking my course."

"The first semester was a disaster inasmuch as I was given an extremely heavy teaching load without assistance, to students who at first underestimated my competence, then couldn't keep pace with their courses. Frankly, as a member of a minority group I suspect that the first-semester students thought I was easy picking (missed classes and so forth). The second semester was a pleasure. I had a different set of students, many of whom asked to be in my courses."

Had a satisfying experience (N = 10):

[It is] always satisfying to teach, reach students, and see a 'gleam in their eyes' as they become more attuned to their environment."

"Teaching well and getting positive feedback from students, both in terms of their performance and evaluations, have been one of the most stimulating experiences of my life."

What effect did these reactions have on the participants' attitudes toward a career in college teaching? The participants' answers to this question, which was asked in the end-of-year questionnaire, are shown in Table 31. In essence, the first year's experiences had a positive effect for 50 percent of the participants, no effect for 30 percent and a negative effect for 20 percent. Several respondents who said that there had been no effect added comments explaining that they already knew they liked teaching as a result of experiences in high school, as a TA, or in college teaching before they began to work on their doctorate.

Several themes emerged from the participants' explanations for their reactions. The most frequent theme was that, although there were problems during the first year, the new teachers expected the situation, their performance, or both to get better in the future:

"I find the idea of teaching very exciting and challenging, but the practice of teaching is often depressing! However, I'm convinced that the first year is the hardest and that I will improve."

"My appetite has been whetted, and I am anxious to improve particular lectures with which I was not satisfied this past year."

Those whose desire to teach increased usually attributed this effect to their enjoyment from working with students and seeing valuable results. Conversely, several participants commented on the difficulties that they encountered with some students:

Table 31. Effect of the First Year's Experiences on Attitude Toward a Career in College Teaching

"What effect have your experiences during the past year had on your desire to be a college teacher?"

Strongly increased	21%	50%
Moderately increased	29%	
No effect	29%	29%
Moderately decreased	14%	21%
Strongly decreased	7%	

"How strong is your desire at this time to continue being a college teacher, relative to other academic roles (research or administration) or to non-academic roles?"

Strong desire to continue	40%	70%
Moderate desire to continue	30%	
No strong feelings either way	7%	11%
Very mixed feelings	6%	
Moderate desire to change	12%	16%
Strong desire to change	4%	

"Lack of interested response from students has hurt."

"The number of mediocre and/or uncaring students at this school is depressing."

"After teaching overseas (England, Sudan Africa, Indonesia) where students were more receptive, courteous, and anxious to learn and be challenged, I have found it harder to adjust to U.S. students than I had anticipated. Students at this institution have to be motivated to learn. Thus, I have to change part of my approach."

Another frequent theme, an echo of earlier comments, was that participants enjoyed teaching but not the other aspects of being a college or university professor:

"It may seem ironic that I am very satisfied with my teaching experience this past year yet still not more excited about being a teacher. My 'psychic satisfaction' with teaching is offset by my disgust with how the university is administered."

"I like teaching but don't know if I'm willing to pay the dues (low salary, exploitation by senior faculty, work on nonteaching or nonresearch chores, and so forth) for the length of time needed to arrive at a tenure position."

Other participants found that they simply did not enjoy teaching, and they were looking at other types of work:

"I found myself bored and unchallenged by teaching this semester, as trite as it sounds. As a result, I have a moderate desire to get into other academic or nonacademic roles."

"I do not find the role of teacher, as my primary occupation identity, satisfying. Also, the financial remuneration is far below what I can earn in other lines of work."

"Many times, I felt that some, if not many, students didn't seem to think about why they are learning and/or what they are learning. It bothered me much throughout the year, and I kept wondering, Why do I want to be a college teacher?"

After determining whether their first-year experiences had increased or decreased their desire to continue teaching, I asked participants what the resulting status of that desire was (Table 31 displays the results). For the large majority (70 percent), the experience of teaching was either satisfying enough or showed promise of becoming satisfying enough to warrant a continued investment of time and effort. Nevertheless, despite the screening procedures

Table 32. Participants' Plans for the Following Year

	Number of Participants
"Expect to get out of teaching altogether and into some other line of work."	11
Is this the result of negative experiences this year?	
Yes	6
No	5
"Plan to stay in teaching but will make the following changes:	83
Change my approach to teaching	17
Spend *less* time relatively on teaching	36
Spend *more* time relatively on teaching	2
Teach more *in* my area of specialization	34
Teach more *outside* my area of specialization	6
Teach more *upper*-division courses	29
Teach more *lower*-division courses	3
Increase my teaching load	13
Reduce my teaching load	9
Maintain the same teaching load	44
"Do not expect to make any changes next year."	3

of graduate schools, one in six new teachers (16 percent) had a moderate or strong desire to get into some other kind of work.

Plans for the Following Year. What were the participants' plans for the following year? How many expected to leave college teaching? For those who stayed, what changes did they plan to make? Participants' responses to these questions are displayed in Table 32.

More than 10 percent planned to leave teaching. However, only half of these said that they were leaving as the result of negative experiences during the first year. It is unfortunate that some of the people in this group had a very good record as a teacher, but they were leaving for other reasons. For example, the person with the highest course evaluation in the whole study was planning to leave, because she was on a one-year contract, and it had not been renewed. The comments of some of the people indicated that they were leaving academia because they were highly attracted to some other kind of work, often in the government. Although they said that they were not leaving because of negative experiences, we can assume that their experiences were not too positive, or they would not have been attracted elsewhere.

Of those who were going to stay in teaching, nearly all expected to make changes of some sort. Many expected to change the type, level, or number of courses that they taught. One in six indicated that they planned to make some changes in the way they taught. Presumably, they saw this as an opportunity to correct the shortcomings they saw during their first year. The comments of those in this group suggested that most of the changes referred to organizational differences (for example, more lecture, less lecture, more and different kinds of exercises), not just content changes.

More than one third of the participants expected or hoped to spend less time on teaching vis-à-vis other activities than they had during the first year. This is somewhat understandable, because their familiarity with the subject matter, students, and so forth had increased by the end of the first year. But, it also suggests that several people were not going to spend much time revising courses that had been put together amid the rush of a very busy first year. This may be the most serious consequence of teacher overload during the first year. Overload forces new teachers to teach in a way that allows or requires the least amount of thought and preparation. Then, the pressures of other duties prevent many from ever revising their courses or learning new ways to teach in subsequent years.

What Else Did They Accomplish?

As everyone in higher education knows — but as outsiders do not always appreciate — college professors are called on to do many things besides teach. At four-year colleges, there are numerous committees to fill. At universities, research and publications are expected. As already noted, 90 percent of the participants in this study attended universities that offered the master's or the master's and doctor's degrees.

What scholarly work did the new professors manage to accomplish in addition to their teaching and committee work? Table 33 shows that they managed to accomplish quite a lot, considering what else they had to do. More

Table 33. Other Scholarly Accomplishments of Beginning Teachers

	Number of Participants
Completed dissertation	34
Articles for scholarly journals:	
• Submitted one or more	49
• Had one or more accepted	22
Research grants:	
• Submitted one or more proposals	39
• Received one or more grants	24
Presentations at professional meetings:	
• Regional	32
• National	52
Served on graduate student committee	33
Other (scholarly writing, committees):	40

than half gave presentations at national meetings, one third finished their dissertation, one fourth wrote journal articles that were accepted for publication, and one fourth received a research grant. Forty percent listed other accomplishments. Writing encyclopedia articles, writing a chapter for an edited book, and preparing lab manuals were among them. As Table 34 shows, the size of the teaching load affected the quantity of other scholarly acomplishments. The new professors who had lighter teaching loads submitted more research proposals and more journal articles, and they made more presentations at national meetings.

Summary

This chapter reviewed the information generated by the study of how the subjects fared as new college teachers—in their own eyes, the eyes of their students, and the eyes of their colleagues.

The teachers' self-perceptions were of course influenced by their own values; these values, while reflecting high expectations, were also rather conservative, as one might expect of people just coming from a graduate school ethos. In fact, the majority of them stated that their approach to teaching was modeled after one or more of their former teachers. This conservative character was reflected in their answers to a number of value questions: They preferred the "principles-and-facts" teaching prototype, desired the "expert" role more than any other role, and thought that the knowledge required for teaching was similar to (rather than different from) the knowledge required to do research.

However, a minority of the subjects did have a different view of college teaching. The difference between the majority and minority groups of teachers showed itself in their respective reactions to the TLGG teaching preparation programs. Those who participated in but did not value the TLGG experience exhibited the conservative value pattern described above. Those who did value

Table 34. Effect of Teaching Load on Scholarly Accomplishments

	Percentage of Participants Who:			
Relative Teaching Load[a]	Submitted Articles	Submitted Research Proposals	Finished Dissertations[b]	Made Presentations at National Meetings
Light	64%	48%	47%	68%
Average	49	42	57	63
Heavy	43	33	64	62
Very heavy	30	20	29	60

[a] These categories were based on the number of courses and the number of different preparations each teacher had.
[b] This figure is the percentage of those who had not finished their dissertations before the year started.

the experience were more inclined to prefer the "student-as-mind" teaching prototype, value the role of "ego ideal" as much or more than the role of "expert," and believe that the knowledge required for teaching was different from the knowledge required for doing research.

Whatever their values were, many of the new teachers had difficulty converting them into effective action. Sometimes this was simply because they did not have the necessary abilities. In other cases it was because of constraints put on them by their new departments. Given the fact that over 55 percent of the participants were given teaching loads that required four-to-eight separate subject matter preparations during the first year, the majority were not able to teach the way they wanted to. What most of the teachers did was resort to the traditional and relatively time-efficient mode of teaching: lectures and readings. The tragic part of this is that, as was seen later in the chapter, many of the teachers did not plan to go back and do a more thorough job of developing their courses because of the pressure from other duties. Hence the mode of teaching that was fashioned in a time-short condition became the dominant and regular pattern for these teachers.

The task of making general statements about the quality of the participants' teaching is complicated, as can be seen in the structure of Table 29. The self-assessment of the new teachers themselves did not always agree with that of their colleagues, which in turn did not always agree with that of the students. To the degree that general statements can be made, it seemed that the new teachers were usually able to establish good relationships with their students and demonstrate good knowledge of the subject matter of their courses. Conversely, they had difficulty as a group in stimulating students to high intellectual effort, changing their teaching approach as appropriate, and involving students. This latter item seemed to be related to not knowing how to lead effective discussions in class. Observations from my site visits suggested that the teachers varied considerably in their ability to read the pedagogical situation and to make contact with students. In terms of overall judgments of performance, it appears that one out of six did quite well even though it was their first year, one half did an adequate job, and one third had problems. This is based on student evaluation scores and on the new teachers' self-assessments.

There was a high degree of variation in the overall performance of the new teachers from course to course. Half of the participants in the study had more than one course or section of a course evaluated with the IDEA instrument. Half of those who had the multiple evaluations received ratings that were very different from course to course or from section to section. The reason for this variation was not clear. One explanation might be that new teachers do not yet have the range of teaching abilities necessary to cope with a wide variety of teaching situations.

As one might expect, this diversity resulted in very different feelings about the teaching experience of the first year. The majority had reactions that were basically positive. But one out of ten had negative feelings and two out of ten had very mixed feelings. As a result, 20 percent had a reduced desire to continue being a college teacher, 16 percent had a moderate or strong desire to leave college teaching, and over 10 percent said they expected not to be in college teaching the next year.

Some of those who were leaving had performed well as teachers but were leaving for other reasons. Of the five who said they were leaving for other reasons, two wanted to do so only temporarily and hoped to return in the future. The other three were making a career shift into planning or other research work. Although their reasons were not always clearly given, they seemed to feel they would simply be happier doing something else.

In general, there appear to be some positive elements in this complicated picture. The majority of the new teachers did a reasonably good job or better, and some of these were taking steps to improve their teaching. However, there are also elements that create concern. A third of the new teachers seemed to have significant problems, a third planned to spend less time on their teaching in the future, and a number were leaving the profession in spite of the fact that they were good teachers.

This study has revealed several problems in the preparation, situation, and performance of new college teachers. The recommendations of the new teachers, made at the end of the first year, are combined with the findings in the study to suggest helpful actions that could be taken by new teachers themselves, by departments receiving new teachers, by graduate students, and by graduate departments.

Summary and Recommendations

L. Dee Fink

The study of nearly 100 beginning college teachers reported in this sourcebook is in essence an in-depth examination of professional entry patterns in higher education. Information was collected on the origin, distribution, preparation, situation, and performance of study participants. This information came from the new teachers themselves, from colleagues, from students, and from site visits by the research director. To the best of my knowledge, the result is the most comprehensive study of beginning college teachers available at this time.

As comprehensive as the study is, however, two qualifications are in order. The first qualification pertains to the varied roles that academics fulfill. Information was gathered about all these functions — research, teaching, and service — but the primary focus was on the teaching role. The other roles were studied primarily for how they affected the teaching role. The second qualification relates to the fact that study participants all represented the same academic discipline. The vast majority of study findings do not appear to be unique to members of this discipline. However, in respect to at least two factors, and possibly to a third, the patterns in this discipline are unique. The first factor is the high proportion of people in the discipline who accept an academic position before they finish their dissertation. In some disciplines, this practice is rare. The second factor is that several graduate departments in the discipline have established teaching preparation programs. These programs gave a sizable minority of study participants an experience that is not at all common in graduate education. The third factor is the frequency with which non–tenure-

L. D. Fink. *The First Year of College Teaching.* New Directions for Teaching and Learning, no. 17. San Francisco: Jossey-Bass, March 1984.

track positions were being offered in the discipline at the time of this study. I have not been able to obtain information on the extent of this practice nationwide. Hence, I do not know whether this discipline is unique in this respect. However, it was possible to examine the effect of all three factors by comparing the experiences and performance of participants affected by them with the experiences and performance of participants who were not.

Summary of Data and Observations

The remainder of this chapter will review the results of the study and present a series of recommendations. The summary of data and observations will be organized around four topics: the origin and distribution of participants, their preparation for college teaching, their situation in their new department, and their performance as teachers. The recommendations will be directed towards beginning college teachers, receiving departments and institutions, graduate students, and graduate departments. At the end of this chapter, I will make a few concluding remarks about the long-term effects of the professional entry patterns observed in this study.

Origin and Distribution. As in most other areas of academia, the majority of study participants were white males between the ages of twenty-six and thirty-five. While the proportion of females was low (12 percent), it was higher for study participants than it is for the discipline as a whole (9 percent). Half of the participants were more than thirty years old, which suggests that they had spent a few years between taking some of their academic degrees to fulfill roles other than that of student.

Most participants began their formal higher education in a four-year state-supported college or university. Only 7 percent received an associate of arts degree before receiving their baccalaureate degree. Approximately two-thirds (63 percent) had majored in geography as an undergraduate. The proportion who attended private institutions remained fairly constant between the B.A. or B.S. degree (23 percent) and the Ph.D. (22 percent). However, as they progressed from one degree to the next, size of the institution at which participants received their B.A. or B.S. degree was 14,500; for the M.A. or M.S., it was 23,000; while for the Ph.D., it was 30,000.

This discipline was marked by a significant influx of doctoral students from outside the United States who went on to accept academic positions. Six of these sixteen returned to their own or another country to teach, while the others remained in this country.

The placement pattern of study participants in their first postdoctoral academic appointment was fairly supportive of the trickle-down theory. Almost all study participants did their doctoral work in a nationally ranked graduate department. One went to a higher-ranked department, and 74 percent went to a slightly lower-ranked department. Only 8 percent went to an institution that had no graduate program.

While there was only a moderate amount of vertical movement downward in terms of status and prestige, there was a great deal of geographical movement. Fifty-seven percent of those who stayed in this country crossed a regional boundary, while 85 percent crossed a state boundary. As already noted, such movement had both professional and social as well as financial implications.

One characteristic of new academic positions in this discipline appeared to be in transition during the time of this study. In the first year of the study (1976–77), 46 percent of the positions accepted by study participants were non–tenure track positions; that is, they were one- or two-year appointments. By the second year (1977–78), the proportion of non–tenure track positions had increased to 63 percent. This factor created considerable insecurity for those who accepted these positions.

The departments claimed to be putting more relative importance on teaching qualifications than on research qualifications in making appointments to new positions. This was true for all categories of institutions. When a distinction was made between tenure-track and non–tenure track positions, this relative priority still held for all categories of institutions except for institutions where the department awarded the doctor's degree. In these institutions, teaching qualifications were still more important for non–tenure track positions than research qualifications, but research was given greater priority in tenure-track positions. Other important characteristics of applicants included whether they possessed the needed subject specialization and whether they were congenial and personally compatible with other members of the department.

In determining the teaching qualifications of applicants, departments relied most heavily on applicant's experience as a teaching assistant, on guest lectures, and on letters of recommendation.

Preparation for College Teaching. The question of how well prepared study participants were for the profession of college teaching can be answered on two levels: the extent of their preparatory experiences and their level of readiness for the activities and responsibilities of college teaching.

It was fairly easy to assess the extent of their preparatory experience. Nearly half (47 percent) had some form of teaching experience prior to entering the doctoral program: 4 percent in grade school, 24 percent in high school, and 33 percent at the college level. Forty-one percent had some form of nonschool teaching experience (for example, Sunday school, sailing lessons, boy scout programs). More than one third (35 percent) had taken one or more education courses. The large majority (90 percent) had had some experience as a teaching assistant, but only half of these had had full responsibility for a course as a TA. More than one third had taught one or more courses at another college while in the doctoral program. A significant proportion (30 percent) had participated in a departmental teaching preparation program in connection with the Project on Teaching and Learning in Graduate Geography.

Participants rated the value of each type of preparatory experience differently. As a group, they rated all forms of teaching experience highly, whether the experience occurred prior to their doctoral program, as a TA, or outside the department as a graduate student. They gave low ratings to their education courses except to those that offered practice teaching. They gave mixed ratings to the departmental teaching preparation programs. In the last case, the variation seems to depend less on the program than it does on the congruence between the educational values espoused in the program and the participant's educational values.

Did these activities prepare the participants adequately for college teaching? A competency-based measure of teaching would be required for a complete answer to the question, and the state of the art of educational evaluation has not yet progressed to that point. However, some partial answers can be given. Participants were asked at the beginning of the year to rate their own ability in several areas of college teaching (for example, lecturing and leading discussions). At the end of the year, they were asked to evaluate their own initial level of development in several aspects of teaching (for example, awareness of different teaching strategies), then to indicate whether that level, high or low, had enhanced or hampered their performance as a techer. In both cases the participants as a group rated themselves fairly high. That is, 75 percent rated themselves as moderately capable or higher on every ability listed.

When a breakdown was made to determine the effect of different types of preparatory experiences on readiness, performance, and satisfaction, almost all experiences had a generally positive effect. Education courses, precollegiate teaching, and teaching outside the department during graduate school seemed to be especially effective. The one major exception to this general pattern was the reaction of participants who had participated in a TLGG program and who had valued that experience. These individuals felt less ready than other study participants, and they gave their performance lower marks than others did. However, both their colleagues and their students gave them relatively high marks for performance. The program apparently had some effect on their performance, but it did even more to raise their expectations and their sense of the possibilities of teaching.

Situational Factors. Once the participants arrived at their new institution, they found themselves in a situation with many variables, all of which affected their professional and personal lives. Six such variables were examined in this study. The first was determined by the participants themselves: whether they had completed their dissertation before accepting the teaching position. One third of the study participants had finished their dissertation before starting to teach, one third finished the dissertation during the first year of teaching, and one third did not. Numerous participants commented on the problems created by unfinished dissertations. Those who had to work on their dissertation during the year and finished it had lower midyear self-evaluations from chairpersons, and they found less satisfaction in their first year as a teacher. Surprisingly, their course evaluations were somewhat higher than those of participants who did not finish their dissertations.

The second variable was the type of position that participants accepted: tenure-track or non–tenure track. As mentioned earlier, the proportion of non–tenure track positions increased dramatically between the first and second years of the study. As a result, 55 percent of the participants in the study had a non–tenure track position. Such positions seemed to have a negative effect on a variety of factors. Participants in a non–tenure track position had slightly lower evaluations from both colleagues and students, they found less intellectual companionship with their colleagues, and they found less satisfaction in their first year as a teacher.

The third variable was the size of the participants' teaching load. Teaching load can be described in several ways. One is class size. Thirty-seven percent of the classes taught by all participants had more than thirty-five students. New teachers who had large classes often indicated that this greatly enlarged their work load and that it sometimes prevented them from teaching as they wanted to teach. The average class size did not vary much by type or size of institution. What did vary was the number of classroom hours per week and the number of separate preparations during the first year. Both were significantly larger in the two-year and four-year institutions than they were in the graduate institutions. The average number of classroom hours per week ranged from seven hours per week in major universities to twelve hours in two-year institutions. The average number of separate preparations during the first year ranged from 3.6 in the major universities to 7 in the two-year institutions. Overall, 55 percent of all study participants had between four and eight separate preparations during their first year. Student evaluations revealed that an increase in the number of separate preparations during a single term had a strong, straight-line negative effect on teaching performance. Participants with only one preparation had an average IDEA score of 44, while those with four preparations had an average IDEA score of 22. An excessive teaching load was also identified as the single most important contributing factor in the sense of overload that 76 percent of the new teachers felt.

The three remaining variables had not been described in the research literature, and they were discovered by the research director during the site visits. The first of these situational factors is identification with the institution. Participants were asked whether the institution in which they were working was similar to or different from the one with which they had identified the most as a student. Participants were distributed fairly evenly along a four-point continuum ranging from very similar to very different. However, 62 percent were working in an instiution that was either somewhat different or very different from the one with which they identified as a student. Participants thought that working in an institution with which they did not identify had a negative effect both on their professional satisfaction and on their performance. The second perception was supported by assessments of teaching performance from students, chairpersons, and colleagues: As the participant's degree of identification with the institution decreased, so did the participant's average teaching evaluation scores.

The second new situational factor concerned the participants' relationships with colleagues. Participants were asked to indicate whether they had found intellectual companionship with their colleagues; that is, whether they had found people with whom they could discuss ideas and professional concerns. One third said yes, one half said only to a limited extent, and one sixth said no. Again, it was their belief that failure to find such companionship had a negative effect on their professional satisfaction and performance. Again, their perceptions were supported by evaluations from students, chairpersons, and colleagues: The less companionship they found, the lower was their average teaching evaluation score.

The third new situational factor was the participants' relationships with students. One aspect of the student-teacher relationship involved the new teachers' perceptions of students' readiness for college-level work. At the beginning of the year, the majority of participants (80 percent) had positive expectations in this regard, but by midyear, between thirty and fifty percent had changed their perceptions for the worse. This was especially true in the areas of writing ability, reading ability, background knowledge, and capacity for abstract thinking. Seventy percent thought that the prevailing academic standards at their current institution were lower than their own standards, and half of the new teachers responded by lowering their own standards.

The other aspect of the teacher-student relationship involved the social similarity or difference between teacher and students. Participants were asked to identify both themselves and the majority of their students in terms of economic background, urban or rural background, national origin, regional origin (if they were from the United States), religious orientation, race, and age. Every participant in the study differed from his or her students in one or more of these seven social characteristics. These social differences seemed to create problems in communicating and relating effectively. For each social dimension except age, teachers who were similar to their students received higher teaching evaluations from students and colleagues than teachers who were different. Furthermore, the effect was cumulative: As the number of similarities increased, so did the teaching evaluation scores.

Their Performance as Teachers. The task of measuring and describing teaching performance is complex, as any educational evaluator knows. This study made an effort to identify the underlying values and purposes that guided the behavior of these new teachers and the instructional strategies and methods that they employed. It used multiple evaluators to assess their effectiveness in different aspects of teaching, and it sought to determine the amount of satisfaction that they received from their experiences of the first year.

In their values, the participants revealed a mixture of idealism and conservatism. When asked to identify the most important thing that they could do for students, far more identified promoting general intellectual growth than teaching mastery of specific subject matter. These general value statements were not empty rhetoric. Different statements were associated with different course objectives selected in the course evaluation process.

The conservative side of these teachers was evident in a number of ways. When asked to rank order the four teaching prototypes developed by Axelrod (1973), more than half (52 percent) chose the knowledge-oriented principles-and-facts prototype over the instructor-centered and student-oriented prototypes. Moreover, when participants were asked to indicate which of the six classroom roles developed by Mann and others (1970) they desired most to fill, they put the role of expert over such roles as facilitator and socializing agent. Finally, almost two thirds (63 percent) thought that the kind of knowledge required for teaching was similar to (rather than different from) the kind of knowledge required for research.

One interesting difference came to light between the values of two subgroups related to the teaching preparation programs that some departments had instituted. The difference was evident between those who had participated in but had not valued their experiences in these programs and those who did value them. Participants in the second group expressed much more liberal and less conventional values than the others. For example, they gave the principles-and-facts prototype a lower ranking and the student-as-mind prototype a higher ranking than the others. The difference in values probably explains much of the mixed response to the teaching preparation programs.

When the new teachers tried to implement their values, they usually turned to one or more of their own teachers for models. Forty percent said that their teaching was modelled primarily on one or two of their own teachers, while another 40 percent said that they had borrowed ideas from several teachers. Only 20 percent said that they were trying to develop an independent approach without much modeling.

Whether the methods that the new teachers used were borrowed or created, they usually turned out to be dominated by lectures, textbooks, and audiovisual aids. There was limited use of other techniques such as field-based research projects, simulation games, and computer-based instruction. A number of constraints seemed to prevent the new teachers from using a variety of techniques: lack of familiarity with different teaching techniques, lack of familiarity with local resources, and time constraints created by heavy teaching loads.

The most complex part of the study involved answering the question of how well as a group the new teachers taught. Evaluations were obtained on various aspects of the teaching process from three sources—the teachers, their colleagues, and their students. In general, both the chairperson and the colleagues gave the new teachers higher ratings than the teachers gave themselves. The student ratings were sometimes higher, sometimes lower than the teachers' self-ratings. The student ratings and the self-ratings both indicated that one sixth of the new teachers performed well above average compared with other, experienced teachers. One half did about average, and one third had problems. In other words, there was a range in their performance, but the distribution was overrepresented in the lower half of the scale.

In general, the new teachers received high marks on establishing good relations with students, on their knowledge of the subject, on interest in self-evaluation, and on making tests that evaluated students for more than memorization. However, new teachers received low marks on stimulating students to high intellectual effort, on being flexible in their teaching approach, on involving students in class, and on leading discussions.

The other major finding about the performance of new teachers was that it seemed to vary widely from class to class. Two or more courses or two or more sections of the same course were evaluated by students for forty-six participants. Of that number, almost half (46 percent) had a range of scores (intrapersonal variation) greater than one standard deviation in the evaluation scores of all teachers in the study (interpersonal variation). This suggests not that the instrument used to assess new teachers' performance was unreliable but that the phenomenon being measured is not stable.

At the end of the year, the participants were asked whether they had received psychic satisfaction, which was defined as positive gut-level feelings, from their experiences during their first year as a teacher. The majority (64 percent) said yes. Ten percent said no, and 20 percent had very mixed feelings. In their comments they noted that their feelings about their teaching varied greatly from day to day and that their feelings depended on the course and on the degree of overload. The year's experiences reduced the desire of 20 percent to continue being a teacher, and they left 16 percent wanting to leave the profession. Ten percent actually planned to leave it. However, half of those in the last group enjoyed teaching, but they were leaving for other reasons, such as expiration of non-tenure track contracts or low salary.

One other problem revealed by participants' comments was that only 16 percent said that they planned to change their approach to teaching during the following year. The rest were limited by the need to attend to other duties. This meant that the majority was going to continue using the strategies and techniques put together in the rush of the first year.

Finally, it should be noted that 79 percent of the participants were working in a major university or in an institution that had some graduate programs. Therefore, although they were new teachers and although many were teaching between four and eight different subjects during the first year, they felt pressure to do research and publish. Many did. Apart from finishing their dissertation, thirty-nine submitted one or more research proposals for funding (twenty-four received one or more research grants), forty-nine submitted one or more journal articles for publication (twenty-two had one or more articles accepted), and fifty-two made presentations at national professional meetings.

Recommendations

At the end of what had been a tumultuous first year for many, the participants were asked what recommendations they would make for all concerned in order to help beginning college teachers. It seemed like an opportune time to ask this question, because their experiences were still fresh in their minds and their hindsight was relatively clear-eyed. Their recommendations plus a few of my own based on study findings, are presented in this section for the four parties involved: new college teachers, receiving departments and institutions, graduate students, and graduate departments.

Recommendations for New College Teachers. The recommendations for new college teachers came from two sources: study findings and participants who had just finished their first year of teaching. The study identified numerous factors that influenced the performance and the amount of satisfaction that new teachers derived from the profession. These factors were translated into questions that new teachers should ask when applying and interviewing for an academic position. All these questions are based on factors that significantly affect the amount of satisfaction that one gains from college teaching. Even if one does not have several places to choose from, one should be aware of these factors, because one may have to adjust to them. The comment of one respondent underscores the importance of these factors: "Choose your place of employment wisely," he said. "Decide first whether you wish to teach or to teach and do research. They are quite different."

Applying

What combination of research and teaching do I want?
Am I willing to start teaching before my dissertation is finished?
Am I open to non–tenure track positions?
How can I document the range and quality of my teaching experiences?
How can I document my effort to learn about teaching?

Interviewing

Institutional information:

Is this institution unique in any way?
Is it similar to or different from the one with which I identified the most as a student?
Does the institution reward high-quality teaching? How?
What resources are available to support teaching?

Department/colleague information:

What kind of person or teacher do they really want?
Are they planning to give me an unreasonably heavy teaching load initially?

Are the people in the department people I can relate to?
Are they willing and able to give me the support that I want and need as a new teacher?
Are the prevailing academic standards ones with which I feel comfortable?

Student information:

How prepared are they for college-level work?
In what ways are they similar to or different from me socially?
Are these differences ones that I can adjust to?

The participants had a number of suggestions for people who had accepted a position. In addition to the emphasis on finishing the dissertation and obtaining information about the pedagogical situation that have already been mentioned, their comments focused on six themes.

1. *Prepare as much as possible ahead of time*

   "Be as prepared as possible, with course outlines, lectures, teaching aids, and so forth. Be ready to go before you begin to teach."

   "Be as prepared as possible. Get ahead so that you are not always a week or less ahead."

2. *Plan to work long and hard as a teacher*

   "Get well rested the summer before, because you are going to work harder that first year than you ever have in your life."

   "Be prepared for a great amount of work. Teaching effectively is a most difficult and time-consuming task."

3. *Be flexible*

   "Be flexible but firm."

   "Prepare well beforehand so you can be flexible in your approach."

4. *Get to know your students*

   "Stay in touch with the students. Always listen to them and watch their reactions. They are better critics than we usually admit."

   "Do not overlook, if teaching introductory level courses, the great gulf there may be between your taken-for-granted general knowledge and the restricted life/world experiences of the ex–high school kids you're going to teach."

5. *Realize that you will make mistakes*

   "In your anxiousness to excel, do not overdo things. Know that you will blow it sometimes and get depressed. Humor and self-confidence are absolutely essential."

   "Try to relax and to avoid letting anxiety get out of control. Expect that many things will not go as planned, and then just roll with the punches and adapt."

6. *Learn about yourself as a teacher and about teaching*
"Get the experience and evaluate it."
"Try to sit in on other teachers' classes."

Recommendations for Receiving Institutions and Departments. The departments and institutions that accept new academics play an important role — perhaps the most important role — in their professional development, because these institutions determine the terms, activities, and context within which basic patterns and attitudes are established. Study data participants' comments will be used to make recommendations for four activities: offering non-tenure-track positions, reviewing and selecting candidates, assigning teaching loads, and offering support.

Offering Non-Tenure-Track Positions. The use of such positions increased dramatically in the discipline during the period of the study. For the majority of positions, the purpose seemed not to be financial but evaluational. Seventy-two percent of the chairpersons said that there was a possibility of retaining a new teacher who had received a non-tenure-track position and that retention depended either on the new teacher's general performance or on the new teacher's teaching ability. Of course, for new college teachers the problem of such contracts is that they introduce an additional quantity of tenuousness and uncertainty into a situation that is already full of unknowns.

Reviewing and Selecting Candidates. There appears to be room for improving the review process of candidates for academic positions. The colleagues of new teachers who participated in this study only used three sources of information in making their decisions about candidates: experience as a teaching assistant, a single guest lecture, and letters of recommendation. There are serious limits on the value of each source: A graduate student's experience as a teaching assistant is often unevaluated, one guest lecture is a poor basis for evaluating the range of abilities needed for effective teaching, and studies indicate that letters of recommendation are often based on secondhand sources of information. A better procedure would be to ask all candidates, first, to document the extent of their teaching experience; second, to provide evaluation information relative to that experience; third, to describe their efforts to develop as teachers. If a department is concerned about identifying particular kinds of teachers, it can request such things as course outlines, videotapes, and essays about teaching and learning.

When selecting new faculty members, department staff should consider their personal and social compatibility with the institution, with other faculty members, and with students. The data from this study suggest that outstanding individuals in the wrong place will probably not perform outstandingly. Whenever compatibility was not considered and the fit was negative, the new teachers' satisfaction with teaching and the evaluations of their performance decreased. Compatibility is not always easy to determine, but to the degree that it can be determined, it should be given serious attention.

Assigning Teaching Loads. When teaching loads are being assigned to new college teachers, three variables need to be considered: the size of the classes, the type of classes, and the number of classes. The new teachers had difficulty with large classes, with lower-division courses, and with a large number of courses. Even after the allowance made by the IDEA data base for class size, the new teachers still had lower course evaluations in large classes. At the end of the year, 40 percent said that they would have been more effective if they could have taught more upper-division courses in their area of specialization. An argument can be made that new teachers just out of graduate school will teach more effectively in upper-division or graduate courses with small numbers of motivated students on topics where up-to-date information is especially valuable. Conversely, more experienced teachers may be able to do a better job with lower-division courses, because they have come to understand students and because they have had time to synthesize broad areas of knowledge.

The biggest problem seems to be the large number of courses assigned to new teachers: Fifty-five percent of the teachers in the study had between four and eight separate preparations for the year. If institutions of higher education want new professors to teach effectively and to develop professionally, this is certainly not how to accomplish it. When the participants were asked to name the single thing that their current department or institution could do to help them the most, the second most frequent response was that their teaching load could be reduced.

"Give me a smaller load to begin with, knowing that all my materials have to be prepared afresh and that I need more preparation time."

"Decrease the diversity of courses I was expected to teach. I'm not Superman, although I was expected to be!"

"Change [my] teaching load—I got bored with four sections of the same course."

A more reasonable approach would be to assign only one or two courses per term during the first year and not more than three different preparations for the year. Assuming that one new course is the work load equivalent of two regular courses, an assignment of the scale just described makes for a more tolerable load. It might also give the new teacher time to explore different methods of teaching or to do other things to develop his or her capability as a teacher.

Offering Support. Although graduate departments can offer some degree of preparation for college teaching, receiving departments and institutions need to provide opportunities for on-the-job training and development as teachers. New teachers might be more motivated to take part at this time than they were when graduate students, especially if participation was coordinated with a lighter teaching load. On the midyear questionnaire, nine participants said that they had taken advantage of programs on college teaching at their new institution and spoke positively about their value. (Two participants were now working in countries other than the United States.) At the end of the year, participants were asked whether they would have opted to attend a well-run discussion seminar on college teaching if their teaching loads had been light enough. Thirty-five percent said that they definitely or probably would have attended, 13 percent said that they definitely or probably would not have attended, 5 percent said they might have attended. Nearly half did not answer the question. This could mean that they were not interested, or it could mean that their teaching load made the question too hypothetical. However, even a 35 percent participation rate would probably be sufficient to support such a program at most institutions.

When the participants were asked to state their single most important recommendation for receiving institutions, 14 percent mentioned increased institutional support for teaching. Such support included audiovisual aids, better classrooms, more flexibility in scheduling, and genuine support for quality teaching. Another critical source of support was at the department and colleague level. When participants were asked whether they would have appreciated more assistance from fellow faculty members, 62 percent said yes (22 percent said very much, and 40 percent said somewhat), and 38 percent said no. When participants were given a list of types of assistance and asked to check the types that they desired, seven types of assistance were desired by 25 percent or more of the respondents:

- Explained the availability of local resources for the support of teaching (for example, audiovisual center, teaching grants)
- Discussed the problems involved in teaching particular courses or in teaching at the institution
- Discussed general problems involved in teaching
- Invited me to their classes to observe, learn, and critique them
- Offered to visit my classes to observe and make suggestions
- Carefully explained the criteria used in salary and personnel decisions
- Invited me to social events

When the participants were asked to make their most important recommendation in their own words, only a few (12 percent) had no suggestions. The others echoed themes that have already been discussed: better information at the start of the year (nineteen mentions), reduction in teaching load (seventeen mentions), improved institutional support for teaching (thirteen mentions), and more feedback on teaching (seven mentions). "Miscellaneous" comments from thirteen participants reflected individual concerns: "Pay me more." "Make this a tenure-track position." "Get rid of the deadwood in this department." In sum, institutions, departments, and colleagues can do a number of things to provide better support for new college teachers that they do not do, presumably either because they do not realize what they can do, or they are not sure that the assistance is really desired.

Recommendations for Graduate Students. The basic message to graduate students was: Make better use of any opportunities that you have to learn about teaching. Stated more fully, the advice is: If you plan to enter the academic profession, you should realize that you will be doing a lot of teaching—probably more than the professors in your own doctoral department. Therefore, it will probably increase your own sense of effectiveness and satisfaction if you learn as much as you can about teaching beforehand. That means taking advantage of opportunities to learn about college teaching as a graduate student.

When participants were asked to state their single most important recommendation for graduate students, four themes were prominent:
- Get more and better teaching experience (mentioned 48 times)
- Learn more about teaching (mentioned 24 times)
- Find out if teaching is for you (mentioned 11 times)
- Finish dissertation beforehand (mentioned 5 times)
- Miscellaneous (13 items)

These themes are illustrated by the following comments:

"If at all possible, teach an entire course or at least guest lecture for someone. Discussions and labs are not the same as lectures."

"Insist on some sort of observation of outstanding or innovative teachers (not necessarily from the same discipline), followed by discussion and analysis."

"Undertake a professional course of teacher preparation."

"Try and get some experience first to see if you really like it."

"Finish your dissertation before starting to teach."

Recommendations for Graduate Departments. Participants were asked what one thing their graduate department could have done differently that would have helped them most during their first year as a teacher. Almost all participants (95 percent) answered this question. Thirty said that their department could have provided more and better teaching experience, twenty-five said that it could have developed their ideas about college teaching, and nine said that it could have provided more feedback on their teaching. Eighteen participants said their graduate school experience was satisfying and made no recommendations.

A few comments can be made on each kind of recommendations. Participants who had no recommendations to make usually did not indicate whether they did not feel the need for help or whether their department had done a lot to help them. Half of these participants had taken part in a departmental teaching preparation program.

For those who recommended more and better teaching experience, in some cases, it meant having some teaching experience, rather than none at all.

In most cases, however, the recommendation for more experience meant that the respondent was calling for the opportunity to be a teaching assistant in different courses with different subject matters, not in the same course each year, while the recommendation for better experience usually referred to being given greater or even full responsibility for a course. As one participant commented, there is a big difference between running a lab section and doing everything involved in developing a course. Here are some typical comments:

> "Require me to do some teaching before I take a job as a teacher."

> "Let me TA different courses, rather than the same ones over and over."

> "Too much grad student time is spent carrying slide projectors and collating exams."

> "Let me actually teach a course or two; that is, give me full responsibility with consultation."

A large proportion of those who said that the department could have developed their ideas about teaching wished that they could have developed their ideas about teaching while in graduate school. They had several suggestions: Offer seminars on college teaching. Hold discussions with outstanding teachers. View videotapes of themselves, or of excellent teachers, teaching. Give lessons on how to handle different types of student. Other respondents wanted information on the nuts and bolts of teaching: textbook selection, teaching tricks, and useful exercises. Here are some typical comments:

> "Any kind of organized discussion or seminar on teaching."

> "Provide videotape sessions and analysis of techniques used by effective teachers."

> "An analysis of teaching methods and materials. I had lots of experience, but I spent a lot of time making mistakes."

> "Spend more time helping develop ideas concerning exam development and course design."

> "Offer a course in methods of teaching geography. There are hundreds of exciting experiments, demonstrations, projects, methods, map exercises, air photo and field things I would have loved to know about."

For those who said that the department could have provided more feedback on their teaching, it was one thing to have teaching experience and another to learn as much as possible from the experience. Thus, a number of participants recognized the value of specific feedback on their own teaching. They envisioned this as coming from students, a TA supervisor, and even a qualified outside evaluator in response to actual classroom observations or to the viewing of videotapes. In every case, the key point was that the feedback must consist of something more detailed than "not bad" or "well done." Here are some illustrative comments:

"I had the opportunity to try my hand at teaching, but I got no feedback."

"More 'teaching' discussions between TAs and instructor."

"Have an expert on teaching methods sit in on a class and evaluate my performances."

"Teaching experience within the department with taping, discussion, and feedback."

In essence, these suggestions support the model of an ideal teaching preparation program presented in Chapter Two as Figure 1. The new teachers in our study recommended all eight activities listed there as well as the four associated functions: providing experience, providing feedback, providing models, and developing one's conceptualization of the act of teaching.

Issues and Opportunities. Any graduate department that is inclined to respond to these suggestions faces a number of issues and opportunities. The first is whether to view available teaching assistantships only as an inexpensive way of meeting heavy departmental teaching loads and providing financial support for promising graduate students or view them also as a way of developing the teaching capability of graduate students. Taking the second view presumably would serve not only to help the graduate students in the future, but it could also improve the quality of their teaching as TAs. The fact that first-year college teachers who had received feedback on their teaching as graduate students did better as teachers than those who did not receive such feedback supports this belief. However, some costs are involved. Taking this view means trying to coordinate assistantships so that each person gets experience in teaching different subjects and gradually receives increased responsibility. It means having someone take the time to observe TAs and give them detailed feedback. Finally, it means having a TA supervisor who holds regular sessions on topics more general than "what do we do Monday morning"?

Another issue is whether to establish a departmental teaching preparation program. Since a program of this nature would presumably involve a seminar and other related activities, it is the most obvious way of responding to the recommendations for readings on college teaching, observations and analysis of excellent teaching, information about the nuts and bolts of college teaching, and opportunity to develop course plans and materials without undue pressure. That such a program is needed seems clear. Certainly, first-year teachers felt a need for better ideas about teaching after beginning to teach. However, graduate students do not always feel a need for such information. Not everyone in this study who participated in a teacher preparation program seemed to teach better as a result. Indeed, it was only those who both participated in such a program and valued the experience who seemed to benefit from it. Those who participated in the program but did not value it seemed to have ideas about teaching that prevented them from taking advantage of the program. Thus, if a department desires to establish such a program, it seems advisable to make participation voluntary. Comments about the existing programs also suggest that the program director needs to be able to gain the respect of participants by raising and dealing with fundamental issues and felt needs, not with superficial problems. The program should not be farmed out to the education department unless the education department program is unusually good. Most study participants who took education courses did not react positively to them.

Still another issue is whether to offer a seminar or set of discussions on the problems and practices of the academic profession. Study participants were often surprised — and not always pleased — by many aspects of being a full-fledged faculty member in an academic department. Many of their miscellaneous comments raised questions that could be dealt with in such a seminar or set of discussions:

"Assisted me more effectively in the job search so it could have been less stressful."

"Made it clear that good teaching would ultimately be rewarded (tenure). Good teaching is now a necessary but insufficient trait for tenure."

"Tell me how to cope with stagnant faculty members."

"Discuss politics and personalities. That has been the biggest thing."

The fourth issue for graduate departments involves opportunities for graduate students to teach courses off campus. Such opportunities are not available everywhere, but study participants who were able to avail themselves of them had one of the highest subgroup teaching scores in the study. Where such opportunities do exist, graduate students should be encouraged to take advantage of them.

The final consideration for graduate departments is the value of the activities just described. In addition to the possibility that such activities can improve the teaching of teaching assistants, these activities could be used to document the ability and development of graduate students as teachers. In an era of stiff competition for academic positions, such documentation would seem to offer candidates a competitive advantage. It could consist of a record of courses in which the student assisted, a list of seminars on college teaching that the student attended, a list of course materials that the student developed, a list of courses that the student taught with full responsibility, and student evaluations, with the changes over time highlighted. A graduate student who entered an interview armed with such documentation should be in a good competitive position.

Long-Term Effects of Entry Patterns

Although the study reported here was restricted to the first year of new college teachers, the patterns observed justify a few reflections about the possible long-term effects of these entry patterns. The first pattern involves the social and cultural mixing for study participants, and that seemed to be good for higher education in general. The study population included several people from foreign countries, and many crossed a regional boundary when going from graduate school to their first academic appointment. Although such transitions seemed to create some communication problems in the short run, this kind of cross-cultural contact should be valuable in the long run.

There was much less mixing among institutional types. Study participants received their doctoral degrees from nationally ranked departments in major universities. Very few began their higher education in two-year institutions, and very few returned to such a college or even to a four-year college. There was very little vertical movement on the prestige hierarchy. If this is true throughout the full range of institutions of higher education, it may explain the communication problems among different types of institution.

The second pattern observed in the study that seems to have major consequences was the clear, widespread condition of overload and uncertainty experienced by the new teachers. The uncertainty was caused by the fact that 55 percent received a non–tenure-track position. For 66 percent, the overload was caused by an unfinished dissertation, and for 55 percent it was caused by a teaching load that required between four and eight different preparations during the first year. If we make the not unreasonable assumption that it takes twice as much time to prepare for and teach a new course as a regular course requires, these new teachers had the teaching load equivalent of eight to sixteen courses — on top of all their other duties.

Given their heavy teaching loads, few new teachers had time to develop an understanding of the process of college teaching by taking a seminar on the subject or by observing the classes of excellent teachers, nor were they able to lay the foundations for future teaching by experimenting with different strategies and techniques. More important, this did not seem to be a temporary problem that was resolved after the first year. Only 2 percent of the respondents thought that they would be able to spend more time on teaching during the following year. Only 9 percent expected a lower teaching load, and only 17 percent said that they would be changing their approach to teaching.

Despite these and other problems, it was also clear that a large majority of the new teachers enjoyed the profession of college teaching. Comments in questionnaires and interviews convinced me that, with only a few exceptions, the study participants had come to enjoy learning and they genuinely wanted to help others to learn. The new teachers' second most desired role was to serve as an ego ideal for students. Both this desire and the hoped for results of teaching were a source of frustration and a mainstay for the new teachers. They were deeply frustrated when they failed to motivate students or they did not "see the lights come on." But, the desire for such results kept them going despite bad days in the classroom and political battles in the department. Thus, both the enjoyment of teaching — the *psychic satisfaction*, as it was called in the study — and the desire to achieve it may be the most precious assets that higher education has in its attempt to fulfill its teaching function.

References

"AAG Membership Profiles." *AAG Newsletter,* 1979, *14* (2), 11.

Axelrod, J. *The University Teacher as Artist: Toward an Esthetics of Teaching with Emphasis on the Humanities.* San Francisco: Jossey-Bass, 1973.

Broeck, J. O. M. *Compass of Geography.* Columbus, Ohio: Merrill, 1965.

Cahn, S. M. *Scholars Who Teach: The Art of College Teaching.* Chicago: Nelson-Hall, 1978.

Caplow, T., and McGee, R. J. *The Academic Marketplace.* New York: Basic Books, 1958.

Eckert, R. E., and Williams, H. Y. *College Faculty View Themselves and Their Jobs.* Minneapolis: College of Education, University of Minnesota, 1972.

Fact Book on Higher Education. Washington, D.C.: American Council on Education, 1977.

Fink, L. D. "Developing Temporary Faculty: The Challenge Posed by Teaching Assistants." *Educational Horizons,* 1976–77, *55* (2), 56–63.

Fink, L. D., and Morgan, D. J. "The Importance of Teaching in Academic Geography." *Professional Geographer,* 1976, *28* (3), 290–298.

Hildebrand, M., Wilson, R. C., and Dienst, E. R. *Evaluating University Teaching.* Berkeley: Center for Research and Development in Higher Education, University of California, 1971.

Hoyt, D. P., and Cashin, W. E. *Development of the IDEA System.* IDEA Technical Report No. 1. Manhattan, Kans.: Center for Faculty Evaluation and Development in Higher Education, 1977.

Lewis, L. S. *Scaling the Ivory Tower: Merit and Its Limits in Academic Careers.* Baltimore, Md.: Johns Hopkins Press, 1975.

McCall, H. R., and others. *Problems of New Faculty Members in Colleges and Universities.* East Lansing: Center for the Study of Higher Education, Michigan State University, 1961.

McGrath, E. J. "Graduate Work for College Teachers." In T. C. Blegen and R. M. Cooper (Eds.), *The Preparation of College Teachers.* Washington, D.C.: American Council on Education, 1950.

Mann, R. D., and others. *The College Classroom: Conflict, Change, and Learning.* New York: Wiley, 1970.

Pattison, W. D., and Fink, L. D. *Preparing Others to Profess: A Trial Year.* Director's Report, Project on Teaching and Learning in Graduate Geography, Phase I (July 1973 to June 1974). (ED 107-552)

Roose, K. D., and Andersen, C. J. *A Rating of Graduate Programs.* Washington, D.C.: American Council on Education, 1970.

Sopher, D. E., and Duncan, J. S. *Brahman and Untouchable: The Transactional Ranking of American Geography Departments.* Discussion Paper Series No. 10. Syracuse, N.Y.: Department of Geography, Syracuse University, 1975.

Wilson, L. *The Academic Man: A Study in the Sociology of a Profession.* New York: Oxford University Press, 1942.

Further Sources

In addition to the publications cited in the preceding report, there are a number of books, articles, and reports that are written either for new college teachers or about new college teachers. In the belief that some readers will be interested in one or both types of materials, these are listed below in separate categories.

Materials for New College Teachers. The scope of the items listed here varies. Some are focused specifically on teaching and offer practical advice for new teachers, for example, McKeachie's *Teaching Tips.* Other are broader in scope and make comments, sometimes rather humorously, on such things as the social and political life of academe, for example, Peddiwell, *The Saber-Tooth Curriculum.*

Cornford, F. M. *Microcosmographia Academia: Being a Guide for the Young Academic Politician.* Chicago: University of Chicago Press, 1972. (Originally published 1922)

Eble, K. E. *Professors as Teachers.* San Francisco: Jossey-Bass, 1972.

Eble, K. E. *The Craft of Teaching.* San Francisco: Jossey-Bass, 1976.

Eble, K. E. *The Aims of College Teaching.* San Francisco: Jossey-Bass, 1983.

Gullette, M. M. (Ed.). *The Art and Craft of Teaching.* Cambridge, Mass.: Harvard-Danforth Center for Teaching and Learning, 1982.

Justman, J., and Mais, W. *College Teaching: Its Practice and Its Potential.* New York: Harper & Row, 1956.

Kolstoe, O. P. *College Professoring, or Through Academia with Gun and Camera.* Carbondale, Ill.: Southern Illinois University Press, 1975.

McKeachie, W. J. *Teaching Tips: A Guidebook for the Beginning College Teacher.* Seventh edition. Lexington, Mass.: Heath, 1978. (Originally published 1951)

Mandell, R. D. *The Professor Game: What Really Goes on in the Multibillion Dollar Education Industry.* New York: Doubleday, 1977.

O'Toole, S. *Confessions of an American Scholar.* Minneapolis: University of Minnesota Press, 1970.

Peddiwell, J. A. *The Saber-Tooth Curriculum.* New York: McGraw-Hill, 1939.

Rothwell, C., and others. *The Importance of Teaching: A Memorandum to the New College Teacher.* New Haven, Conn.: The Hazen Foundation, 1968.

Udolf, R. *The College Instructor's Guide to Teaching and Academia.* Chicago: Nelson-Hall, 1976.

Materials about New College Teachers. Academics have been concerned about the recruitment, preparation, and support of college teachers for a long time. This list contains some of the more prominent works on this topic during the last fifty years.

Axelrod, J. (Ed.). *Graduate Study for Future College Teachers.* Washington, D.C.: American Council on Education, 1959.

Berelson, B. *Graduate Education in the United States.* New York: McGraw-Hill, 1960.

Blegen, T. C., and Cooper, R. M. (Eds.). *The Preparation of College Teachers.* Washington, D.C.: American Council on Education, 1950.

Clark, M. L. *An Exploratory Study of Graduate Assistantships and an Assessment of the Value of These Assistantships for Beginning College Teachers.* Doctoral dissertation, Columbia University, 1963.

115

Dean, D. S. *Preservice Preparation of College Biology Teachers: A Search for a Better Way.* Washington, D.C.: Commission on Undergraduate Education in the Biological Sciences, The American Institute of Biological Sciences, 1970.

Diekhoff, J. S. *Tomorrow's Professors: A Report of the College Faculty Internship Program.* New York: The Fund for the Advancement of Education, n.d. (circa 1960).

Dunkel, H. B. "Training College Teachers." *Journal of Higher Education,* 1958, *29,* 1-7.

Gray, W. S. *The Training of College Teachers.* Chicago: The University of Chicago Press, 1930.

Kline, M. *Why the Professor Can't Teach: Mathematics and the Dilemma of University Education.* New York: St. Martin's Press, 1977.

Koen, F., and Ericksen, S. C. *An Analysis of the Specific Features Which Characterize the More Successful Programs for the Recruitment and Training of College Teachers.* Ann Arbor, Mich.: The Center for Research on Learning and Teaching, The University of Michigan, 1967.

McGrath, E. J. *The Quantity and Quality of College Teachers.* New York: Institute of Higher Education, Bureau of Publications, Teachers College, Columbia University, 1961.

Monson, C. J., Jr. "Teaching Assistants: The Forgotten Faculty." *Educational Record,* 1969, *50* (1), 60-65.

Nowlis, V., Clark, K., and Rock, M. *The Graduate Student as Teacher.* Washington, D.C.: American Council on Education, 1968.

Salyard, A. B. *An Approach to Preparing Teaching Assistants for College and University Teaching.* Master's thesis, University of California at Los Angeles, 1973.

Wahlquist, J. T. *Innovations in the Preparation of College Teachers.* Bloomington, Ind.: Phi Delta Kappa, 1970.

Yuker, H. E. *Faculty Workload: Facts, Myths, and Commentary.* ERIC Higher Education Research Report #6. Washington, D.C.: American Association of Higher Education, 1974.

Index